ISLANDS THROUGH TIME

ISLANDS THROUGH TIME

A Human and Ecological History of California's Northern Channel Islands

Todd J. Braje, Jon M. Erlandson, and Torben C. Rick

ROWMAN & LITTLEFIELD
Lanham • Boulder • New York • London

Published by Rowman & Littlefield
An imprint of The Rowman & Littlefield Publishing Group, Inc.
4501 Forbes Boulevard, Suite 200, Lanham, Maryland 20706
www.rowman.com

86-90 Paul Street, London EC2A 4NE

British Library Cataloguing in Publication Information Available

Library of Congress Cataloging-in-Publication Data

Names: Braje, Todd J., 1976- author. | Erlandson, Jon, author. | Rick, Torben C.,
author.
Title: Islands through time : a human and ecological history of California's northern
Channel Islands / Todd J. Braje, Jon M. Erlandson, and Torben C. Rick.
Other titles: Human and ecological history of California's northern Channel Islands
Description: Lanham : Rowman & Littlefield, [2021] | Includes bibliographical
references and index. | Summary: "Islands Through Time tells the remarkable story
of the human and ecological history of California's Northern Channel Islands. The
resilience of the Chumash and Channel Island ecosystems provides a story of hope
for a world increasingly threatened by climate change, declining biodiversity, and
geopolitical instability" —Provided by publisher.
Identifiers: LCCN 2021038827 (print) | LCCN 2021038828 (ebook) | ISBN
9781442278578 (cloth) | ISBN 9781442278585 (epub)
Subjects: LCSH: Channel Islands (Calif.)—History. | Natural history—California—
Channel Islands. | Human ecology—California—Channel Islands. | Chumash
Indians—California—Channel Islands. | Channel Islands (Calif.)—Antiquities. |
Channel Islands National Park (Calif.)
Classification: LCC F868.S232 B73 2021 (print) | LCC F868.S232 (ebook) | DDC
979.4/91—dc23
LC record available at https://lccn.loc.gov/2021038827
LC ebook record available at https://lccn.loc.gov/2021038828

ISBN: 978-1-4422-7857-8 (cloth : alk. paper)
ISBN: 978-1-5381-8802-6 (pbk. : alk. paper)
ISBN: 978-1-4422-7858-5 (ebook)

♾™ The paper used in this publication meets the minimum requirements of
American National Standard for Information Sciences—Permanence of Paper for
Printed Library Materials, ANSI/NISO Z39.48-1992.

Islands through Time is dedicated to the Chumash people who have called the Northern Channel Islands and the greater Santa Barbara Channel area their home for millennia, and still do. We honor the fact that the islands—known to the Chumash as *'Anayapax*, *Limuw*, *Wima*, and *Tuqan*—are the ancestral homeland and tribal territory of the Chumash people. We are privileged and humbled to work on the Channel Islands and to study the deep history of the Chumash people and the remarkably beautiful land and sea they have inhabited for so long.

CONTENTS

ACKNOWLEDGMENTS

We are grateful for contributions to the book by Courtney H. Buchanan, Alicia Cordero, Sue Diaz, Kristina M. Gill, Michael Glassow, Amy Gusick, Courtney A. Hofman, Kristin M. Hoppa, Martha Jaimes, Mena Moreno, Daniel Muhs, Jan Ward Olmstead, Jennifer Perry, Leslie Reeder-Myers, Deborah Sanchez, Georgiana Sanchez, Diane Valenzuela, Veronica Vasquez, René L. Vellanoweth, and Luhui Isha Waiya.

We are indebted to a variety of friends, colleagues, and mentors who have helped shape our thinking about Channel Islands archaeology, ecology, and natural history. At Channel Islands National Park, we thank Lulis Cuevas, Russell Galipeau, Kristin M. Hoppa, Ann Huston, Laura Kirn, Ethan McKinley, Kelly Minas, Don Morris, Mark Senning, Stephen Whitaker, and Ian Williams for all their help with field research and their willingness to share their vast knowledge of the Channel Islands. At the Nature Conservancy, Jennifer Baker, Christie Boser, David Dewey, John Knapp, Scott Morrison, Eamon O'Byrne, and John Randall have been instrumental in our research on Santa Cruz Island and for interpreting Channel Islands ecology. At the Smithsonian, we thank Terry Chesser, Rob Fleischer, Jesus Maldonado, Kathy Ralls, and Scott Sillett for their collaborations on island projects. At the University of Oregon, several academic generations of graduate students have contributed to a deeper understanding of the island's history, including Amira Ainis, Scott Byram, Molly Casperson, Deana Dartt, Eric Forgeng, Tracy Garcia, Nicolas Jew, Tony Largaespada, Rob Losey, Susan Norris, Mark Tveskov, René Vellanoweth, Lauren Willis, and Jason Younker.

One of the things that makes the Channel Islands so special is the rich community of researchers who work on their cultural and natural history. We thank all our friends and colleagues who have helped shape our thinking, including Jeanne Arnold, Julie Bernard, Paul Collins, Roger Colten, Robert DeLong, Kate Faulkner, Lynn Gamble, Kristina Gill, Mike Glassow, Anthony Graesch, Amy Gusick, Dan Guthrie, Courtney Hofman, Brian Holguin, Chris Jazwa, John Johnson, Doug Kennett, Mike Macko, Sharon Melin, Dan Muhs, Kathryn McEachern, Ken Niessen, Seth Newsome, Peter Paige, Jennifer Perry, Leslie Reeder-Myers, Dan Richards, Sam Spaulding, Heather Thakar, Jan Timbrook, Larry Wilcoxon, and many more, who we have met on boat rides to the islands, at island research stations, or at the California Islands Symposium.

We thank the members of the Chumash community who have worked with us or advised us over the years as consultants, colleagues, and tribal monitors. This includes Alicia Cordero, Sue Diaz, David Domingues, Mark Alow Garcia, Quintan Shup Garcia, Larry "Goose" Garnica, Brian Holguin, Martha Jaimes, Kote Lotah, Mena Moreno, Jan Ward Olmstead, Paula Pugh, Alan Salazar, Deborah Sanchez, Georgiana Sanchez, John Ruiz, Alan Thiessen, Julie Tumamait-Stenslie, Gil Unzueta, Diane Valenzuela, Veronica Vasquez, Matt Vestuto, Luhui Isha Waiya, and many others. We also thank the Santa Ynez Band of the Chumash Indians Elders Council for their continued support through the years. We thank them for their willingness to work with us and share knowledge of their rich cultural heritage and the legacy of the Chumash past, present, and future on the Channel Islands.

Finally, we thank our families for their support, especially while we were away on the islands.

I thank my wife, Sopagna, and my son, Ellis, for all their support, encouragement, and patience.

Todd J. Braje

I thank Kristina Gill, my sons, Erik and Robert, and my late parents, Robert and Patricia, for many years of support.

Jon M. Erlandson

I thank my wife, Kelsey, and my daughters, Luella and Willa, for all their support. I also thank my parents (Gary and Linda) and my sister, Hadley, for first introducing me to the Channel Islands and supporting me throughout that journey.

Torben C. Rick

PREFACE

With sparkling blue ocean waters and relative isolation, few places are as intriguing or beautiful as California's Channel Islands. A short boat or plane ride from the mainland whisks one away from the hustle and bustle of modern American life into a different world that offers glimpses of what ancient California might have been. For us, Channel Island trips have always been a refreshing escape from our daily lives, where we immerse ourselves in their wonder and beauty.

We are honored to have had the opportunity to study the human and natural history of the Channel Islands for many years. We appreciate the trust shown to us by the Chumash community, Channel Islands National Park, The Nature Conservancy (TNC), and other partners. For Braje, this is a journey spanning more than a decade of research that built on his early work in Florida and a childhood in Indiana. Growing up in Ventura, California, Rick was hooked on the Channel Islands from an early age and became fascinated by their archaeology as an undergraduate at the University of California at Santa Barbara in the 1990s. Erlandson, born and raised in Santa Barbara and surfing, swimming, and sailing the waters of the Santa Barbara Channel, has studied the archaeology of the islands for more than 40 years. Together, with many colleagues and collaborators, we forged foundational knowledge of the

Channel Islands while graduate students (Braje and Rick) and a faculty member (Erlandson) at the University of Oregon. When island tourists were surprised that we came all the way from the Pacific Northwest for research, we were always quick to describe the amazing archaeological history and ecological legacy of the islands. Sometimes described as "California's Galápagos," they are known worldwide in scientific circles. We have always been amazed by what the islands can teach us and what they still hold for the future.

The vast majority of our knowledge and interpretations of the human and ecological histories of the Channel Islands are published in academic papers, edited scientific volumes, and books intended for a narrow audience of scholars and researchers. These can be difficult to access and follow, a chore to decipher without years of training in academia. Our research, however, is most often accomplished with publicly funded grants and contracts, and we believe it is important to share what we have learned with a broader audience—with the hikers, boaters, fishers, tourists, and lovers of nature and history who share our passion and fascination with the Channel Islands. This book is our attempt to do this and to show the deep connections among the past, present, and future on the Northern Channel Islands.

To all the readers of this book, thank you! We hope it fans a spark, deepens your interest in the Channel Islands, and helps you see the islands, and our planet, from a new perspective. The millennia-long history of humans is written into archaeological sites, which often rest beneath our feet. This nonrenewable, precious record has a great deal to tell us about human-environmental interactions of the past, present, and future. For the Northern Channel Islands, this is primarily the story of the Island Chumash and their ancestors, which spans more than 13,000 years and continues today.

1

ISLANDS THROUGH TIME

Located as little as 20 kilometers (about 12 miles) off California's southern coast, the Northern Channel Islands include Anacapa (Chumash name: *'Anyapax*), Santa Cruz (*Limuw*), Santa Rosa (*Wima*), and San Miguel (*Tuqan*) (figure 1.1). The islands are part of a larger archipelago that includes the Southern Channel Islands of San Clemente (Gabrieleño-Tongva name: *Kinkipar*), Santa Catalina (*Pimu*), Santa Barbara (*Tchunashngna*), and San Nicolas (*Haraasnga*). Although similar in many ways, the northern and southern islands have somewhat different cultural and geological histories (textbox 1.1). On clear days, you can see all the northern islands from the mainland—shimmering visions of green and brown, their rugged mountain peaks seemingly rooted in the depths of the Pacific Ocean. They are a siren call for nature lovers and anyone seeking refuge from the hustle and bustle of southern California. Just an hour or two drive and a short boat trip or plane ride from downtown Los Angeles, the islands offer a trip back in time before strip malls, skyscrapers, freeways, and other developments came to dominate modern American life.

The Northern Channel Islands are a treasured part of the National Park System. You will find no convenience stores, gas stations, hotels, restaurants, or other modern amenities on the northern islands, but you will discover a unique array of plants and animals, at least 145 of

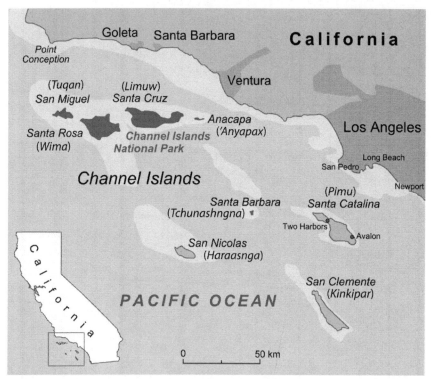

Figure 1.1. Map of the southern California Bight and the Northern and Southern Channel Islands. Chumash names for the northern islands are provided in parentheses, as are Gabrieleño-Tongva names for the southern islands. *Source:* **open access image.**

which are found nowhere else on Earth. Isolation and evolution created numerous one-of-a-kind species on these relatively small islands. Despite the lack of giant tortoises and marine iguanas, the islands have been called the American Galápagos for their distinctive flora and fauna and natural* beauty.

Most tourists who step foot on the Northern Channel Islands feel as though they have been transported back in time to a pristine California. Rocky headlands, sandy beaches, rolling hills, grassy tablelands, and other habitats are more secluded and less affected by the anthropogenic changes that have altered the mainland. One glimpse of the diminutive

---

* The term *natural* implies a disconnect between people and the planet's ecosystems, climate, and lifeforms. We use the term here to refer to the physical world and life other than humans. However, humans are explicitly a part of nature, helping to shape the "natural" world for thousands of years.

Textbox I.I. Size, Distance to Mainland, and Age of Earliest Confirmed Human Occupation for Each of California's Channel Islands

Although this book focuses on the Northern Channel Islands, which were once united into the super island Santarosae and are found in Chumash territory, the Northern Channel Islands are closely related to the Southern Channel Islands in Gabrieleño-Tongva territory. Some of these connections are highlighted in this book. Here, we list the basic statistics on the current size, distance from the mainland, and age of earliest known human occupation for each island (with size and distance following Schoenherr et al.'s *Natural History of the Islands of California*°).

Northern Channel Islands (Santarosae)

San Miguel Island: Chumash name: *Tuqan*. Size of landmass: 37 square kilometers. Distance from mainland: 42 kilometers. Age of earliest human occupation: ~13,000 years ago (based on earliest radiocarbon dates for Santarosae at the Arlington Springs site).

Santa Rosa Island: Chumash name: *Wima*. Size of landmass: 217 square kilometers. Distance from mainland: 44 kilometers. Age of earliest human occupation: ~13,000 years ago.

Santa Cruz Island: Chumash name: *Limuw*. Size of landmass: 249 square kilometers. Distance from mainland: 30 kilometers. Age of earliest human occupation: ~13,000 years ago.

Anacapa Island: Chumash name: *'Anyapax*. Size of landmass: 2.9 square kilometers. Distance from mainland: 20 kilometers. Age of earliest human occupation: ~13,000 years ago.

Southern Channel Islands

San Nicolas Island: Gabrieleño-Tongva name: *Haraasnga*. Size of landmass: 58 kilometers. Distance from mainland: 98 kilometers. Age of earliest human occupation: >8,000 years ago (based on presence of chipped stone crescents).

Santa Barbara Island: Gabrieleño-Tongva name: *Tchunashngna*. Size of landmass: 2.6 square kilometers. Distance from mainland: 61 kilometers. Age of earliest human occupation: >4,400 years ago (based on earliest radiocarbon dates).

Santa Catalina Island: Gabrieleño-Tongva name: *Pimu*. Size of landmass: 194 square kilometers. Distance from mainland: 32 kilometers. Age of earliest human occupation: >8,000 years ago (based on presence of chipped stone crescents).

San Clemente Island: Gabrieleño-Tongva name: *Kinkipar*. Size of landmass: 145 square kilometers. Distance from mainland: 79 kilometers. Age of earliest human occupation: ~9,000 years ago (based on earliest radiocarbon dates).

° Allan A. Schoenherr, C. Robert Feldmeth, and Michael J. Emerson, *Natural History of the Islands of California* (Berkeley: University of California Press, 1999).

island fox (*Urocyon littoralis*) or the shy Channel Island spotted skunk (*Spilogale gracilis amphiala*) or crossing paths with the brilliant purple and white flowers of the Santa Cruz Island bush mallow (*Malacothamnus fasiculatus suppnesioticus*) or the rare perennial herb Greene's dudleya (*Dudleya greenei*) drives this idea home (figure 1.2). In reality, however, the Channel Islands have changed dramatically during a long human history that spans at least 13,000 years.

Many of these alterations were driven by natural climatic changes and geological events, but many more resulted from human influences. Less than 300 years ago, the Northern Channel Islands were occupied by thousands of Chumash people living in large coastal villages, fishing in kelp forests, foraging in the intertidal zone, and collecting a variety of plants from coastal plains and upland terraces (figure 1.3). For millennia, Indigenous peoples shaped island ecosystems and adapted to tremendous climatic and landscape changes, including global warming and

Figure I.2. Endemic fauna and flora from the Northern Channel Islands: (A) an island fox; (B) a spotted skunk; (C) a flower from the Santa Cruz Island bush mallow; and (D) Greene's dudleya. *Source:* open access images via wikimedia.org.

rising seas. They altered plant and animal communities by introducing mainland species, burning landscapes, and managing local resources. The descendants of the Island Chumash maintain their connections to the islands today, playing an active role in understanding island resources of the past and present, and preserving their cultural heritage for the future.

The Chumash and the Islands

Written by Alicia Cordero and Luhui Isha Waiya (Channel Islands National Marine Sanctuary Advisory Council, Chumash Community Seats) and Georgiana Sanchez, Sue Diaz, Martha Jaimes, Mena Moreno, Deborah Sanchez, Diane Valenzuela, Veronica Vasquez, and Jan Ward Olmstead (Chumash Women's Elders Council).

For Chumash people, the Channel Islands and the surrounding National Marine Sanctuary hold a value that is beyond measure. We originate from the islands themselves. The island and marine ecosystems co-evolved with our ancestors and our culture. Chumash maritime culture has been and continues to be intimately shaped by that connection. Even though we have been dispossessed of our islands and surrounding waters, we always have been and will always be here. We are here in the ecosystems shaped by untold generations of Chumash traditional tending. We are here as protectors of the buried ancestors and villages. And we are here through the prayers of our people longing for reconnection with our ancestral home. Our relatives exist here too—dolphins, foxes, oaks, *Olivellas*, abalone. The Chumash people *are* the islands and the waters. Tending that relationship is the collective birthright and sacred responsibility of all Chumash people. Our cultural, spiritual, psychological, and physical well-being depend on meeting that responsibility. The islands remember our people. The lands and waters have been in intimate relationship with the Chumash people for millennia and that trajectory will continue into the future far longer than the lifespan of any individual or government. The value of that enduring relationship is truly too great to be described with words.

The Chumash people originate directly from this region in deep time. The oldest human remains documented in North America were found on the Channel Islands and are estimated to be about 13,000 years old. For temporal perspective, this Chumash ancestor lived on the large island of *Santarosae* before it was divided by sea level rise into the modern Channel Islands. Using standard estimates of average human generation time, seafaring people have been living along the mainland and islands of the Santa Barbara Channel for more than 520 generations. Over these millennia, California's flora, fauna, and even the land and waters have developed and changed together with its people. The Chumash peoples, including our culture, values, cosmology, lifeways, epistemologies, and languages have thus emerged specifically from the lands and waters of the Santa Barbara Channel and have continued to develop and change in relationship with them.

All the abundance that has shaped and sustained Chumash people and society for thousands of years has been provided by our traditional lands and waters. To this day, Chumash ancestors and ancient villages are still present underground, below the ocean itself, and in the minds, hearts, traditions, and oral histories of living Chumash people. Held within Chumash cosmology is a fundamental gratitude to the land, waters, and living beings of this area for our existence, sustenance, and wellness. Embedded in this gratitude is a sacred responsibility to protect, care for, and live in deeply knowledgeable, reciprocal, and regenerative relationship with these relatives. Chumash traditional ecological practitioners (as well as a growing number of mainstream biologists) understand that the islands and their surrounding waters are intertwined systems with species interdependency, which blurs the boundaries between the aquatic and terrestrial.

Me'pšumawiš a tipašumawiš (Together we are healthy and spiritually at peace).

After the Chumash were removed by Spanish missionaries or forced to abandon their island homes in the early 1800s, fishermen, hunters, and travelers frequented the islands. Their visits were relatively brief, but they too altered the islands, leaving permanent footprints on island ecosystems. Beginning in the 1850s, the islands were used primarily as ranches and farms that exported wool and meat from sheep and cattle, wine, fruit, grains, and nuts to California and beyond. Commercial ranching transformed the islands and left an indelible imprint on island plants, animals, soils, hydrology, and more. In the buildup to World War II and the Cold War, the US military took possession of portions of the archipelago as part of their coastal defense system. The structures and landscape modifications they left behind are still prominent features on certain coastlines and ridge tops.

Figure 1.3. Marine organisms on the Northern Channel Islands: (A) shellfish such as abundant California mussel beds on San Miguel Island; (B) rich, dense giant kelp forests; (C) seals and sea lions such as northern elephant seals; and (D) marine birds such as the American oystercatcher. *Source:* Image A by Todd J. Braje; images B, C, and D are open access images via islapedia.com.

In 1938, Anacapa and Santa Barbara islands were declared a National Monument, and in 1980 all the Northern Channel Islands and Santa Barbara Island were incorporated into Channel Islands National Park. The Nature Conservancy owns the western two-thirds of Santa Cruz Island, however, and the US Navy still owns San Miguel Island. In 1980, the Channel Islands National Marine Sanctuary was established and protects 1,252 square nautical miles of water surrounding the islands, and a network of marine reserves and no-fish zones were created in 1999. All these agencies, despite different agendas and goals, are actively engaged in resource protection, conservation, and restoration efforts.

A central mission that binds them together is a focus on the maintenance of biodiversity and the preservation and restoration of natural systems. Archaeological and paleoecological research, ethnographies, oral histories, and other sources of deep historical information are taking center stage in driving this mission forward by improving our understanding of long-term changes in island ecology and biodiversity and guiding conservation management decisions. Records of ecological, climatic, and anthropogenic change spanning millennia increasingly provide insights for contemporary conservation decisions. Restoring and protecting the fragile ecology of the islands must include an understanding of what they looked like in the past.

This is a sea change for modern conservation management and science. Only in the last decade or so have scientists and managers truly integrated deep historical perspectives into their understanding of contemporary ecosystems. History and archaeology matter in much more tangible ways than as simply a means to avoid the mistakes of yesteryear. This book is the story of the deep human and ecological history of the Northern Channel Islands, as well as the relevance of understanding the past for living in the present and planning for the future. Through the lenses of archaeology and historical ecology, we chronicle the amazing history of the Northern Channel Islands, from their geological formation to the arrival of humans at least 13,000 years ago, and the dramatic cultural and environmental changes that have swept across the islands since then. Ultimately, we show why and how this deep history is critical to understanding, interpreting, and protecting the exceptional natural and cultural resources of the islands today and into the future.

ISLANDS OF CHANGE

Islands hold a deep allure. For scientists, explorers, sailors, or tourists, these seemingly isolated worlds in the sea conjure images of sandy beaches, brilliant sunsets, and places frozen in an idyllic state. When Captain Cook and other European explorers sailed the globe, they "discovered" many islands—large and small, temperate and tropical—most already inhabited by Indigenous peoples living in small worlds with strange plants and animals. Travel logs detailing their adventures fascinated the European public, and the modern myth and allure of islands took shape. Charles Darwin's famous voyage of discovery aboard the HMS *Beagle* and his colorful descriptions of the unusual plants and animals of the Galápagos Islands helped spawn the fields of island ecology and biogeography (the distribution of plants and animals through space and time). Darwin and, at practically the same time, Alfred Russel Wallace, in the Malay Archipelago, observed related yet uniquely different plants and animals on various islands, leading them to develop the theory of biological evolution via natural selection.

What often is lost on casual observers is that even the most isolated islands on Earth, separated by seemingly impassible water barriers, have been and are in a constant state of flux. At a small scale, this happens every day. The sun rises and marches its way across the sky, temperatures fluctuate, and plants and animals respond in kind. Tides ebb and flow as gravity forces the oceans to bulge in the moon's changing direction and beaches and rocky shores shift in character. At a slightly longer scale, the tilt of Earth on its rotational axis away from or toward the sun creates distinctive seasons in its year-long orbit. Birds migrate, plants bloom, fish spawn, and a delicately complex symphony of ecological changes takes place. In the natural world, the daily, seasonal, and annual fluctuations of ecosystems shape our days, weeks, months, and years.

If we consider island evolution beyond the scales of a human lifetime, much more dramatic and unpredictable changes take shape. During the past 2.6 million years, variations in the amount of insolation (the intensity and timing of heat from the sun) resulted in at least five Ice Ages. During cold periods, glaciers expanded, pulling water from the oceans and revealing new islands and land bridges as sea levels retreated and new coastlines of existing islands and continents were exposed. The rising and falling of sea levels, combined with shifts in regional rainfall and aridity, dramatically changed the size and shape of the islands (see chapter 2) and created prominent landscape features. These and many other natural climatic changes helped shape and reshape island environments around the globe. In many cases, contemporary island ecosystems only resemble their ancient selves in the broadest of terms.

By extending our temporal lens back into geological time over hundreds of thousands to tens of millions of years or more, contemporary island landscapes often become unrecognizable or nonexistent. Some islands formed millions of years ago when the supercontinent of Pangaea broke apart through the process of continental drift. Chunks of land, such as Australia and Madagascar, drifted away from continental landmasses and became islands. Even when landforms did not fully separate, continental drift combined with rising sea levels sometimes resulted in the formation of new islands and island chains when low-lying land bridges flooded. In other cases, oceanic islands formed through the eruption of volcanoes on the ocean floor, with lava flows building up until they broke through the water surface. Such processes not only occurred deep in the past but also continue to produce new islands or add to existing islands today. Anyone who has visited the Hawaiian Islands and witnessed an active volcano spewing lava into the ocean has seen this geological activity play out on a small scale. Other island types formed as barrier, tidal, or coral islands and were constructed over thousands to millions of years through geological processes of sedimentation, erosion, and uplift. The natural activities that formed these islands lent a set of distinctive characteristics that helped shape the natural and cultural histories that followed.

Humans have been another major source of island change, and the heavy hand of recent human activity is hard to miss on many islands around the world. This is obvious when you visit islands with large populations and major tourist industries. For the thousands of honeymooners lucky enough to spend their holiday on Tahiti or Hawai'i, for example, bustling airports, modern skyscrapers, and lavish hotels with luxuriant amenities await the happy couples. The human footprint on land and seascapes is hard to escape in such major ports of call. As honeymooners migrate out to romantic bungalows and sandy beaches along island fringes, however, it can feel like a trip back in time to a natural and pristine world, largely free from human engineering.

In some ways this is true. The seemingly pristine places in our world like national parks, wildlands, remote mountain peaks, protected rainforests, and uninhabited deserts are refuges for plants and animals and, often, hot spots for biodiversity. They offer places of solace, reflection, and escape from our bustling cities and stressful lives, and a connection to what the world was like before the entanglements of industrialization, globalization, and exploding human populations. The sobering reality is, however, that every place on the planet and realm of nature has been fundamentally altered by humans. Even the seemingly pristine beaches of the Pacific and Caribbean have been transformed. Many of the plants and animals of the Hawaiian Islands—pigs, chickens, dogs, rats, pineapples, bananas, and many more—were introduced by humans.[1]

Many of these introductions occurred centuries before Captain Cook arrived in Hawai'i, carried by Polynesian voyagers who brought a suite of domesticated plants and animals to help them survive on this remote archipelago. Introductions have been even more dramatic in the last several centuries of European conquest and colonialism, when hundreds of invasive plants and animals were introduced and spread across Hawai'i and other islands around the globe, purposefully and accidently. Exotic species have fundamentally reshaped island ecologies, but many casual observers now view them as part of the "natural" world.

This is even true out your own back door. Many familiar and seemingly American plants are recent immigrants: eucalyptus trees were introduced from Australia for lumber, fuel, and windbreaks; exotic European dandelions and crabgrass regularly battle homeowners in the war for the perfect lawn; and the iconic tumbleweed of the cowboy American West is a Russian thistle. We tend to have a short memory when it comes to our surroundings. It can take less than a generation or two for an introduced plant or animal species or for an ecological shift to become normalized. When an environment changes, we tend to quickly accept the new state as the way things have always been. Most of us evaluate the health of our environments by the yardstick of our own experiences. The state of the world when we were children or young adults becomes the standard by which we measure all subsequent changes.

THE PAST AS PROLOGUE

On the surface, this may seem inconsequential. Slowly or rapidly, everything is always changing. Over time, however, people gradually lose knowledge about the natural world and tend to forget the changes taking place. University of British Columbia biologist Daniel Pauly called this the "shifting baselines syndrome," a revolutionary concept in conservation management.[2] Due to "historical amnesia," we often forget how much the natural world has been degraded by our actions. Our baselines have shifted. Such shifts fall into two main categories: personal and generational. Personal amnesia is when people fail to remember how things used to be during their own lives. You might not notice, for instance, that birds and frogs once common in your own backyard are rare now. Generational amnesia is when information is lost from one generation to the next. A forest that you consider pristine wilderness is viewed in the same way by your children, despite the loss of biodiversity, the introduction of exotic species, and degradation from one generation to the next.

Among environmental scientists, baselines are essential reference points for evaluating the health of ecosystems. They are standards by which we measure change. Baselines are how the world used to be: oceans filled with tunas and large sport fish; tall grass prairies teeming with American bison; skies darkened by flocks of migrating passenger pigeons. Ideally, we set our ecological baselines at reference points prior to heavy human impacts such as industrial-scale fishing that has depleted the world's oceans of much of its bounty, the 16th-century blitzkrieg of bison for their skins, and the 19th-century extinction of passenger pigeons for cheap meat.

Even scientists fall victim to the shifting baselines syndrome. Some scientists tend to accept the stock sizes and species compositions they observed early in their careers as the baseline for evaluating subsequent changes.[3] Historical accounts of phenomenal abundance and even data collected by early scientists are often viewed skeptically by leaders in the field. When new models and methods are developed, older data tend to be viewed as inadequate, which places ever greater emphasis on recent datasets. The result is a gradual shift in baselines and flawed reference points for evaluating the state of ecosystems. Historical amnesia shifts our perception of what is natural toward more and more degraded standards—a disaster in slow motion. With widespread historical amnesia, it is difficult for conservationists to convince people the environment is degraded and that we need to do something about it.

One way to combat such problems is to study places that have been less affected by human activity. Unfortunately, there are very few such places left on Earth. Extreme high-altitude environments or inhospitable deserts may offer insights, but most of the degraded environments in need of restoration are the ones most "useful" and attractive to humans. Most of these have been heavily affected by humans, but largely uninhabited islands such as the northwestern Hawaiian Islands shed some light on the incredible toll modern commercial fishing has taken on our oceans.[4] When their fish populations are compared to those of the main Hawaiian Islands, the results are shocking. Large, carnivorous fish (the most commercially desirable species) made up only 3 percent of fish biomass around the main Hawaiian Islands but 54 percent around the remote northwestern Hawaiian Islands. We have become so numb to an ocean depleted, polluted, and overfished that the productivity was unimagined.

Where else can we look to help overcome the shifting baselines syndrome? The answer, and the way forward, is by looking to the past. Historical sources offer a variety of baselines with which to measure the current state of the world; they are road maps to help us understand how we arrived at the state we are in today and provide perspectives on where we might be headed in the future. Translating historical information into conservation assets is not without challenges. Until recently, most ecologists and biologists overlooked historical data (such as archaeological excavations or historical records) and their potential relevance for modern resource management. For example, an archaeological shell midden (an ancient refuse pile) can tell us about what types of plants and animals were available to people in a given location at a particular time in the distant past (figure 1.4). The shell midden may never provide an environmental inventory of local plants and animals comparable to modern surveys conducted by a botanist or biologist, but historical perspectives can help us reach important truths about past, present, and future worlds.[5]

A variety of academic disciplines study the past and gather deep historical data. These are collected using different methods and offer an array of insights into past ecological conditions at different time scales—from decades, to centuries, to millennia. Living memory, oral histories, and fishing and hunting records, as well as written historical accounts and archaeological, paleontological, and genetic data, all offer important data sources.[6] Each has strengths and weaknesses with differential availability and preservation, often making collection and integration challenging. At times, deep historical information can be at odds with one another and, at others, offer similar perspectives on the state of past ecosystems. Scientists and managers must make difficult decisions on how to integrate these perspectives, evaluate their reliability, and judge their validity. That is why it is essential to integrate as many

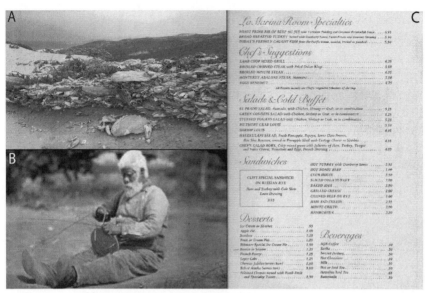

Figure 1.4. Some of the anthropological and archaeological sources of historical ecological information about the past: (A) archaeological shell middens (*source:* Todd J. Braje); (B) ethnographic and ethnohistoric information sources and traditional knowledge such as Chumash consultant Fernando Librado (*source:* open access image via islapedia.com); and (C) historical documents such as bills of fare (menus) (*source:* open access image).

diverse datasets as possible and draw on interdisciplinary perspectives to reconstruct past ecosystems and help build realistic baselines for future restoration targets and goals.

Efforts to integrate perspectives from the past into our understanding and interpretation of modern and future land and seascapes have spawned the relatively new and growing field of historical ecology. The term *historical ecology* has been used by a variety of disciplines such as ecology, geography, and anthropology with various meanings since at least the first half of the 20th century. All agree, however, that the concept references the complex interconnections between history (time), nature, and humans.[7] In the last several decades, historical ecology has expanded and blossomed into an interdisciplinary field of study, focused on adding a deep time dimension to ecology and restoration biology and unified by the idea that history is of vital importance to nature conservation.

The past, however, can be hazy, and gaps can challenge our ability to reconstruct the puzzle of history. It is not always possible to trace, for example, the abundances and distributions of species over thousands of years. For example, building accurate counts of whale populations in the vast Pacific Ocean, even today, is challenging. How, then, can historical ecologists do so through deeper time? Historical records (e.g., logbooks, maps, catch records, early travel journals), archaeology (whale bones in middens or trash piles), and paleontology (ancient DNA, fossil deposits) all help fill gaps, provide clues about ancient populations, and can be compared against modern tallies. These deep historical perspectives offer critical perspectives for evaluating the health and viability of modern populations.

Let's be clear about the goals of historical ecology. The past is gone, never to return. Rewinding the clock to some idyllic, lost ecological state is not the goal; such aspirations are impossible and, in many cases, undesirable. History, archaeology, and paleontology offer avenues for reconstructing slices of the past and answering questions about how we arrived at the modern ecological state, but we will never fully re-create it. In this sense, the goals of historical ecology are to understand how we arrived at present conditions and to provide perspectives and context that can help guide us to where we would like to be in the future.

HISTORICAL ECOLOGY AND THE NORTHERN CHANNEL ISLANDS

California's Northern Channel Islands are one place where historical ecology is taking center stage in guiding conservation efforts on land and sea. Over the last 10 years or so, island managers, archaeologists, biologists, and other scientists and stakeholders have come together to integrate historical perspectives into creative solutions for restoring Channel Island ecosystems. The result has been a better understanding of just how "natural" the islands are today, the legacy of deep history in shaping island environments, and how to better manage island landscapes and seascapes in the future.

This book is the story of the archaeology and historical ecology of the Northern Channel Islands as we understand them today. Using broad strokes, we trace the deep history of the islands prior to human arrival all the way to the present. Our goal is not simply to tell a good story (although that is important) but also to highlight the incredible changes the islands have undergone, naturally and culturally. Ultimately, we show how this history is relevant to managing the invaluable resources of the islands. First and foremost, however, this book is a story about the Island Chumash people, the rich archaeological record they left behind, and the legacy and cultural traditions that continue today and must be preserved into the future. If you have visited any of the Northern Channel Islands, you were in the homelands and waters of the Chumash, where they thrived for millennia and still do.

To fully understand this history, we start in the deep geological past, before even the first appearance of anatomically modern humans in Africa. In chapter 2, we explore geological evidence that illustrates how the islands were formed and the tremendous changes to island landforms and ecosystems over the last several million years. This sets the stage for first human colonization in the late Pleistocene, when the islands looked very different from what they do today. In chapter 3, we tackle some of the most perplexing questions in American archaeology: when and how people first settled the Americas. In just the last 20 years, our understanding of who the first Channel Islanders were and where they came from has fundamentally changed. The Northern Channel Islands contain one of the largest and most significant clusters of Paleo-coastal sites in the Americas and data critical for our understanding of the peopling of the New World.

In chapters 4 and 5, we explore dramatic cultural and environmental changes that took place on the Northern Channel Islands during millennia of Native American occupation, including growing human populations, the establishment of permanent settlements, numerous technological innovations, artistic elaboration, subsistence changes, and the establishment of long distant trade networks. During the last 3,500 years, rapid and pronounced cultural and environmental changes swept the islands and the Island Chumash. Stemming from small colonizing groups of hunter-gatherers just 10,000 years earlier, the Chumash established intensive trade networks, with craft specialists, a market economy, and an amazingly complex sociopolitical system. We explore how these changes occurred during some of the most unstable climatic conditions of the last 10,000 years, and how the Chumash survived and thrived in such tumultuous times.

We continue the story in chapter 6 when Spanish explorers made first landfall on the Channel Islands in 1542 CE, an event that ushered in a new era for the Chumash. Over the next 300 years, Spaniards colonized the adjacent mainland, disease epidemics swept through Island Chumash villages, the survivors were forced to move to mainland towns and missions, and the islands were transformed into privately owned ranches and fishing outposts. Those three centuries also saw dramatic changes to island flora, fauna, and landscapes as they were transformed into the islands we experience today.

Finally, in chapter 7, after recounting the long history of cultural and ecological change on the Northern Channel Islands, we return to the topic of how archaeology and historical ecology can contribute to current restoration efforts, help protect rare island flora and fauna, and cope with the impacts of climate change on natural and cultural resources. In doing so, we stress the importance of preserving and protecting cultural resources, which today are threatened by rising seas, coastal erosion, and other destructive processes. Ultimately, the history of the Northern Channel Islands is a parable that demonstrates the importance of natural and cultural resources in our modern world and how we might better preserve and protect them for generations to come.

2

ASSEMBLING SANTAROSAE

In the beginning, there was only darkness . . . and a slow rain of plankton, pollen, and fine sediments on the deep seafloor off the west coast
of a continent that would one day be known as North America. This
gradual deposition in deep waters was punctuated by occasional volcanic flows and submarine landslides. Roughly 400 million years ago, the
North American plate began to move slowly westward, propelled by
tectonic forces that eventually created the Atlantic Ocean, the North
American continent, the Sierra Nevada and Rocky Mountains, and the
Pacific Coast as we know them today. The leading margin of that continental plate marked the edge of an ancestral Pacific Coast situated east
of its current location. Being on the leading edge of a moving continent
creates dramatically different landscapes than riding along near its
center or trailing edge. The complex geological history of the Channel
Islands reflects their creation and evolution near the dynamic continental margin, at or near the intersection of land and sea.

Today, the four Northern Channel Islands—Anacapa (*'Anyapax*),
Santa Cruz (*Limuw*), Santa Rosa (*Wima*), and San Miguel (*Tuqan*)—
are separated from one another and the adjacent mainland by straits
several miles wide. As little as 11,000 years ago, however, lower sea
levels united the islands into a single and much larger island known as
Santarosae. How Santarosae and the Northern Channel Islands came to

be is the topic of this chapter. The unique east-west orientation of the islands and the Santa Barbara Channel, which separates them from the mainland coast, influences a variety of geographic factors—the relative isolation of the islands, the semi-protected and highly productive waters that surround them, and the presence of unique plants and animals that have led some to call them the American Galápagos.

This unique and dynamic landscape was home to the Island Chumash and their ancestors for millennia. To understand how the Chumash survived, adapted, and thrived on relatively small islands for more than 13,000 years, we must dive into the deep geological history of those islands. This fascinating story will set the stage for what the islands looked like when people first explored and colonized them. It also helps us understand the challenges the Island Chumash faced in adjusting to global and local changes in climate, landscapes, and ecosystems, including a warming climate, rapid sea level rise, and marine erosion that threaten coastal and island communities around the world today.

TECTONIC LEGACIES

Some rocks in southern California are more than a billion years old, but the oldest exposed on the islands today are no more than about 200 million years old. Most are much younger. A quick look at a map of the mountains of western North America, from the Coast Ranges to the Rockies, shows that almost all trend north to south. The Rocky Mountains, for example, stretch for some 3,000 linear miles (~4,800 kilometers) from northern British Columbia to New Mexico. The Northern Channel Islands, however, are a western extension of the Santa Monica Mountains, one of several east-to-west trending mountain ranges in southern California known as the Transverse Ranges. The unusual orientation of the Northern Channel Islands and Transverse Ranges is the result of plate tectonics and enormous geological pressures still unfolding today.

For tens of millions of years, the continental and lighter North American Plate has moved inexorably westward, propelled by plate tectonics. That process created a widening Atlantic Ocean east of North America and caused almost unimaginable collisions off the Pacific Coast. For millions of years, the denser and oceanic Farallon and Pacific plates were forced under the North American Plate.[1] This "subduction" created a deep submarine trench off the California Coast, similar to offshore trenches found today around much of the Pacific Rim and its Ring of Fire. As it moved westward, the North American Plate skimmed sediments off the seafloor and welded them onto the leading edge of a slowly growing continent. Roughly 25 million years ago, however, the last of the Farallon Plate was driven into the deep trench off the west coast and recycled into the Earth's mantle.

The North American Plate then contacted the oceanic Pacific Plate, and their edges began to slide along one another in opposite directions as the mighty San Andreas Fault began to form. To the south, the Gulf of California and Sea of Cortez opened; to the north, a slice of the continent was sheared off and transported to the northwest, fracturing and rotating blocks of Earth's crust under immense pressures. One of these blocks included the ancestral Transverse Ranges—originally oriented north-to-south—the northwest end of which was anchored by the "Big Bend" in the San Andreas, causing it to rotate clockwise roughly 90 degrees. These processes gradually transported coastal terranes west of the San Andreas as much as 200 miles (~320 kilometers) to the northwest. Some rock units found on the Northern Channel Islands today are nearly identical to formations of the same age located near San Diego and the Mexican border.

Before about 30 million years ago, the Northern Channel Islands and the southern California Coast as we know them did not exist. The islands consist primarily of sandstones, shales, and volcanic rocks of mostly marine origin. This suggests that, for the most part, the "islands" were not islands at all but, instead, sediments deposited on the seafloor off the ancient continental margin. For much of the Miocene (23 million to five million years ago), tectonic forces stretched (extended) the crust, creating a unique continental borderland marked by a series of ridges and troughs reminiscent of the Basin and Range topography of western North America. In places, the crust thinned, weakened, and cracked, leading to massive underwater volcanic flows. Elsewhere in deep offshore basins, thick sequences of mostly fine marine sediments were deposited, including several sandstone formations deposited by massive underwater landslides. In others further from the ancient coast, even finer sediments accumulated, including the Miocene Monterey

Formation, which covers as much as 62,000 square miles (~100,000 square kilometers) of southern California's coastal area, both onshore and off—an area roughly half the size of Nebraska. Some of these sediments are rich in organic matter, and their decay under heat and pressure created deep oil reservoirs and surface tar seeps used by humans for millennia for a variety of purposes, from caulking canoes and sealing baskets to building roads and fueling our cars. Other layers were rich in fine silts, clays, and the skeletons of tiny plankton (diatoms and radiolarians) that lived and died in the ocean. These deep-sea sediments can be seen today in the thinly bedded, white- or buff-colored shales of the Monterey and Bechers Bay formations, widespread on Santa Cruz, Santa Rosa, and San Miguel islands. Some are rich in silica that formed beds of hard cherts used by the Chumash to make stone tools for millennia (sidebar 2.1).

Stone, Asphaltum, and Freshwater Resources of the Northern Channel Islands by Jon M. Erlandson, University of Oregon

Archaeologists have long viewed freshwater and other raw materials as available in limited quantities on the Channel Islands compared to the mainland. This notion may have grown out of a need to explain a massive Island Chumash industry devoted to making shell money beads that facilitated intensive trade between islanders and mainlanders [see chapter 5]. Was this trade and bead-making fueled by scarce island resources?

Recent surveys suggest that island resources were more than adequate to support the Island Chumash for millennia. Perhaps the most important was freshwater, with the islands often described as especially prone to cyclical droughts. Island vegetation recovering from more than a century of grazing suggests, however, that fog drip combed by plants from dense island fogs significantly supplements annual rainfall, especially during the "dry" (foggy) summer season.

Another example is chert, a form of quartz used to make stone tools. It was once thought that the only high-quality island chert sources were on eastern Santa Cruz. Today, chert sources are known from every island, and several are abundant and of excellent quality—allowing islanders to make remarkably fine tools. Coarser volcanic cobbles were also widely used to make more expedient tools.

Some of the islands are also rich in sandstones that were fashioned into a variety of ground stone tools—by laboriously pecking away the unwanted material with picks made from local volcanic rocks. Stone bowls were made from "cannonball" sandstone concretions, and some villages on San Miguel specialized in making such bowls, probably for trade to island and mainland neighbors.

Asphaltum was another important mineral for the Island Chumash, used as a glue, sealant, and to caulk plank canoes. Some archaeologists have argued that high-quality asphaltum had to be obtained from the mainland, but large masses and clumps of pure asphaltum regularly wash up on island shorelines from offshore oil seeps.

The Island Chumash had rich raw material resources, but they still traded for obsidian, fused shales, and cherts found on the mainland. Today, many archaeologists view these trade items as novelties or elements of value-added composite goods (arrows, etc.) that made sense for island and mainland peoples to exchange. Much of that trade may have been driven less by necessity, however, and more by the social and political benefits of maintaining contacts, marriage networks, and alliances.

Miocene volcanic eruptions on land and beneath the sea also deposited thick sequences of lava or intrusive igneous rocks that were incorporated into Channel Island terranes. Anacapa Island is made up almost entirely of such volcanic rocks, as is most of northwestern Santa Cruz Island. The northwest coast of Santa Cruz is marked by high, sheer, and rugged sea cliffs cut into these volcanic rocks, testifying to both the erosive power of the ocean and the comparative resistance of hard volcanic rocks to such forces (figure 2.1). On eastern Santa Cruz Island, in an area known as the Contact Zone, volcanic flows deposited on top of siliceous rocks of the Monterey Formation created a series of outcrops of high-quality cherts that were used by the Island Chumash to make millions of small stone drills used to pierce *Olivella* shell money beads fashioned from a marine gastropod, the purple olive snail.

In contrast to the Miocene, rocks dating to the Pliocene (~five million to 2.6 million years ago) are poorly represented on the islands, suggesting that erosion was the dominant process. About four to five million years ago, tectonic pressures building along the San Andreas Fault's Big Bend compressed Earth's crust along much of the southern California coast, creating numerous faults, mountain ranges, and deep basins or valleys. For several million years, erosion in the mountains

Figure 2.1. Massive basalt cliffs of northwest Santa Cruz Island formed by Miocene-age volcanic eruptions. *Source:* **Jon M. Erlandson.**

deposited vast accumulations of sediment in these coastal or offshore basins. In the Ventura Basin north and east of the Channel Islands, as much as 24,000 feet (~7,300 meters) of sediments have accumulated in the last four million years, roughly half of them during the Pliocene. In the depths of the Santa Barbara Basin separating the islands from the mainland, a rain of fine particles continues today, forming thin seasonal beds (known as varves) that span tens of thousands of years. The study of cores taken from these finely stratified sediments has provided remarkably detailed records of changes in climate, ocean temperatures, and animal and plant populations over millennia.

The Pleistocene (~2.6 million to 11,700 years ago) is famous for its dramatic climatic and environmental oscillations, its large suite of now extinct mega-mammals, and the evolution and spread of our human ancestors around the world. During the Pleistocene, a series of cold glacial periods and warmer interglacial cycles occurred, with vast ice sheets repeatedly forming and melting in northern North America, Europe, and other areas of the world. During cold periods, so much water was locked up in glacial ice that global sea levels dropped almost 400 feet (~120 meters). During interglacial periods, including the relatively warm Holocene Epoch we live in today, the melting of glaciers raised global sea levels to roughly modern levels. About 125,000 years ago, at the height of the last interglacial, sea levels were as much as 20 feet (6 meters) higher than today.

Fluctuating sea levels profoundly shaped the geography of the islands and the continental shelves that surround them. The "stairstep" topography visible on many parts of the islands are the remnants of Pleistocene marine terraces, some of which have also been mapped on the submerged landscapes around the islands. Look at many island shorelines today, especially along wave-swept rocky coasts, and you will see how marine erosion created these ancient terraces (figure 2.2). The heavy wave action typical of the islands today slowly cuts what geologists call marine abrasion platforms, nearly flat landforms visible during low tides that are typically backed by nearly vertical sea cliffs of varying heights. Numerous marine terraces formed by the same processes are visible on the islands today, the relatively level terraces being ancient marine abrasion platforms (usually blanketed by younger sediments) and the terrace risers that separate them marking the location of ancient sea cliffs and shorelines.[2] The level top of eastern Anacapa Island is a classic example, visible from the mainland on a clear day, of a table-like landscape planed flat by marine erosion. At 861 feet (253 meters) above sea level, the relatively flat top of San Miguel Hill is another example, one of the higher and older marine terraces on San Miguel and the other Northern Channel Islands.

Associated with the cyclical rise and fall of Pleistocene seas, marine wave erosion also carved numerous caves along dynamic island coastlines. Waves smashing against ancient shores and sea cliffs differentially attacked faults or other weak zones in bedrock, creating caves and overhangs large and small. Some of the larger sea caves provide dramatic experiences for modern visitors to the islands, including the enormous Painted Cave cut almost 440 yards (400 meters) into the tall basalt cliffs along Santa Cruz Island's northwest coast. On calm days, tour boats as much as 60 feet long motor passengers more than 275 yards (~250 meters) into the depths of Painted Cave—accompanied by the sounds of the surging sea and barking sea lions—an experience that must also have enthralled people in smaller boats for millennia. Numerous smaller caves and rock shelters exist on the islands, especially on Santa Cruz and Santa Rosa, and many of these provided the Chumash and their ancestors shelter for domestic and, occasionally, ritual activities.

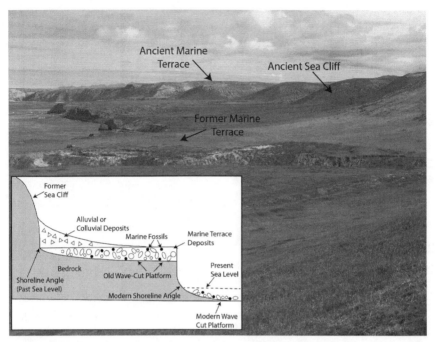

Figure 2.2. Photograph of the coastal landscape on Santa Rosa Island. In the foreground is the grass-covered surface of an ancient marine terrace dated to about 120,000 years ago. Inset: A diagram depicting the wave-formed landscape, common on the Northern Channel Islands. *Source:* **open access image.**

Extensive mapping and dating of island marine terraces by geologists show that, at times, all but the highest island peaks were beneath the sea. At other times, the islands were much larger than today and coalesced into a single island. The discovery of numerous mammoth fossils on the islands once fueled theories that a land bridge connected the Northern Channel Islands to the mainland during the Pleistocene. Seafloor mapping and other subsequent research has shown that no such bridge existed, but that the distance between the mainland and the islands was reduced to a relatively narrow strait about 4–5 miles (7–8 kilometers) wide. University of Illinois geographer Donald Johnson first noted that elephants are very good swimmers and proposed the now widely accepted idea that mammoths swam from the mainland to the islands, potentially at multiple points in geological history (sidebar 2.2).

Were Humans and Mammoths on the Channel Islands at the Same Time? by Daniel Muhs, U.S. Geological Survey

One of the most intriguing questions in Channel Islands research is whether humans and mammoths were on the islands at the same time. The question is important because it bears on the issue of how mammoths became extinct. The cause of the extinction of mammoths on the Channel Islands, as with extinctions of Pleistocene megafauna elsewhere in North America, has been hotly debated. Hypotheses include abrupt climate and vegetation change, loss of land area due to sea level rise, mass extinction due to catastrophic impact from an extraterrestrial body, and extirpation by humans, either through hunting and/or transmittal of disease. These causes are not mutually exclusive, so it is possible that two or more combined to bring about mammoth extinction.

Mammoths almost certainly reached the islands by swimming, likely during glacial periods when lower sea levels decreased the distance between the mainland and the islands. Findings from Santa Rosa Island suggest that such migrations likely happened at least twice, probably during both the penultimate (~160–140 ka [thousands of years of ago]) and last (70–20 ka) glacial periods.[3] During interglacial periods, sea level rose and mammoths likely were stranded on the islands where they experienced a reduction in size.

As of this writing, there is no clear *stratigraphic* evidence of humans and mammoths coexisting on the Channel Islands. Based on the youngest reliable calibrated radiocarbon ages on both charcoal and bone, mammoths lived near Garañon Canyon on Santa Rosa Island until about 13,000 years ago.[4] The oldest human remains at Arlington Springs, also on Santa Rosa Island, have a similar age of about 13,000 years ago, with stratigraphically associated charcoal dating to about 11,600 years ago, and associated rodent bone dated to about 13,400 years ago.[5] Consistent with these ages, the oldest shell middens on San Miguel Island date to between 12,000 and 12,200 years ago.[6] Based on these lines of evidence, it is possible, but not definitive, that humans and mammoths were on the Channel Islands at the same time.

Humans likely entered North America from Asia *prior* to the classic 13 ka Clovis model. One hypothesized route for a pre-Clovis migration is travel along a marine resource–rich Pacific coastal route between ~20 ka and ~15 ka.[7] If this hypothesis is correct, then it is possible that humans encountered mammoths on the Channel Islands several thousand years prior to the youngest dated mammoth remains found thus far (figure 2.3).

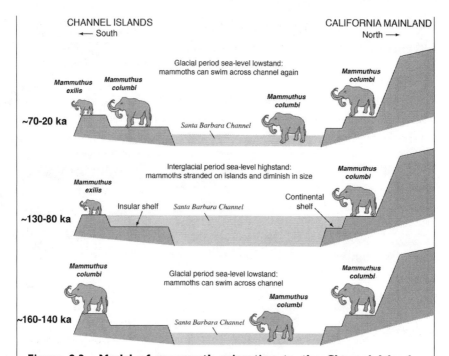

Figure 2.3. Model of mammoth migration to the Channel Islands. Lower panel: Columbian mammoths (*Mammuthus columbi*) migrate to the Channel Islands by swimming during the penultimate glacial period, roughly 160–140 kilo annum, with a lowered sea level and shortened mainland-to-island distance. Middle panel: during relatively high sea levels of the last interglacial period (~130–80 ka), mammoths become stranded on the islands and experience size reduction to a new species, *Mammuthus exilis*. Upper panel: during the last glacial period (~70–20 ka), again with a lowered sea level, a second migration of *M. columbi* to the islands takes place, resulting in a mixed population of *M. columbi* and *M. exilis* on the Channel Islands. *Source:* Daniel Muhs.

Near the end of the Pleistocene, a powerful ice age buried northern North America beneath a massive ice sheet extending from the Pacific to the Atlantic and the Arctic oceans. This massive glacier extended into Washington and New York states and completely covered the Great Lakes region. No glaciers formed on the Channel Islands or in coastal California, which were a refuge for Pleistocene plants and animals during this Last Glacial Maximum (LGM). At the height of the LGM (~23,000 to 18,000 years ago), sea levels were roughly 360 feet (110 meters) lower than today, and the Northern Channel Islands coalesced into a single island known as Santarosae (figure 2.4). At 78 miles (125 kilometers) long, Santarosae was roughly four times larger than the islands are today, with a land area of 830 square miles (~2,150 square kilometers).[8]

When Pleistocene sea levels were lower, including the LGM, extensive sand dunes built up on San Miguel and Santa Rosa islands, the remnants of which can still be seen today. The Pleistocene dunes, made up mostly of tiny calcareous (rich in calcium carbonate) marine shell fragments, weathered and leached over the millennia and created impermeable hardpan layers of calcium carbonate at their base and often formed fossil "caliche forests" of root casts (rhizoconcretions), occasional tree stumps, and other bizarre soil formations that were exposed during later periods of erosion. The cemented remnants of parallel Pleistocene dune ridges and swales form a particularly prominent part of the landscape on

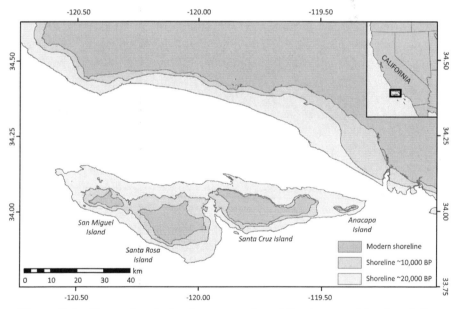

Figure 2.4. Reconstructed paleogeography of Santarosae Island and the southern California mainland at 10,000 and 15,000 years ago. Terminal Pleistocene and Early Holocene archaeological sites are not included on the map due to the sensitive nature of site locations, but all such sites have only been located on the subaerial portions of the Northern Channel Islands. No archaeological sites yet have been located on the now submerged portions of Santarosae Island. Source: Leslie Reeder-Myers.

western San Miguel and Santa Rosa islands, where they can obscure the underlying bedrock and marine terrace features. Similar to the younger dunes on the islands, most of the Pleistocene dune ridges are oriented from northwest to southeast, suggesting that the strong northwesterly winds that batter the islands much of the year have a very deep history. The irregular topography of such dune fields also created numerous poorly drained swales and basins that hosted seasonal wetlands and lakes during wetter periods. Such wetlands—rarely seen on the islands today due to the recent history of heavy grazing, erosion, and climate change—attracted migrating geese and ducks that were important resources for some of the first Islanders.

ORIGINS OF A UNIQUE FAUNA AND FLORA

Near the end of the Pleistocene, southern California's mainland coast was the home of the famous Rancholabrean fauna, including a variety of large mammals (megafauna) that went extinct about 13,000 years ago. These include the saber-tooth cat (*Smilodon fatalis*) and American lion (*Panthera atrox*), a giant short-faced bear (*Arctodus simus*), mammoths (*Mammuthus columbi*) and mastodons (*Mammut pacificus*), bison (*Bison antiquus*), shrub-ox (*Euceratherium collinum*) and wood ox (*Bootherium bombifrons*), the western horse (*Equus occidentalis*), camels (*Camelops hesternus*), giant ground sloths (*Megalonyx jeffersonii*, *Nothrotheriops shastensis*, and *Paramylodon harlani*), a large tapir (*Tapirus californicus*), the dire wolf (*Canis dirus*), and other large mammals.

On the Northern Channel Islands, in contrast, the only large land mammals were the full-sized and pygmy mammoths that roamed the islands until about 13,000 years ago. A single toe bone of a giant short-faced bear was recently identified at Daisy Cave on San Miguel Island and dated to about 17,000 years old, but it is it is likely that the lone bone was deposited by a scavenging bird like an owl, eagle, or condor.[9] It is not clear why more of the large mainland mammals never reached the islands, especially given that the distance between Santarosae and the mainland was much smaller at the LGM and some mainland species such as bears, deer, and elk are relatively strong swimmers.

Prior to the arrival of humans, terrestrial animals were limited to the mammoths discussed earlier, a "giant" deer mouse (*Peromyscus nesodytes*) only slightly larger than its mainland kin, and several species of bats, lizards, snakes, and a salamander. The giant deer mouse and a vampire bat (*Desmodus stockii*) are now extinct on the islands. We don't know precisely when a few other mammals arrived on the Northern Channel Islands, but they may have predated human arrival or arrived after human colonization, including the island spotted skunk (*Spilogale gracilis amphiala*) and the now extinct ornate shrew (*Sorex ornatus*) and San Miguel Island vole (*Microtus miguelensis*). Island land bird communities are also rich and diverse, including bald eagles (*Haliaeetus leucocephalus*), the island scrub jay (*Aphelocoma insularis*), barn owl (*Tyto alba*), and island loggerhead shrike (*Lanius ludovicianus anthonyi*). The shells of land snails, especially *Helminthoglypta ayresiana*, are found in Pleistocene deposits and, although rarely seen alive on the islands today, are abundant in some dunes on San Miguel Island. A variety of insects are also native to the islands—including a small venomous scorpion (*Vejovis minimus thompsoni*), ants, crickets and grasshoppers, a cicada, moths and butterflies, wasps, beetles, and flies—but we know little about their deeper history.[10]

Because of the lack of large terrestrial predators on Santarosae, the island supported a much wider array of marine animals that nest or give birth on land, including a variety of seabirds still found on the Channel Islands today, a flightless sea duck (*Chendytes lawi*) that is now extinct, and six species of seals and sea lions that range from relatively small harbor seals (*Phoca vitulina*) to massive elephant seals (*Mirounga angustirostris*). Sea otters (*Enhydra lutris*) were another important marine mammal on the Channel Islands, and a wide variety of porpoises, dolphins, and whales are found in deeper island waters. The ocean waters around the islands were somewhat cooler during glacial periods, but there were extensive kelp forests and other nearshore habitats that would have supported a similar and very rich array of fish, shellfish, and seaweeds. Kelp forest and other nearshore fishes, like rockfish (*Sebastes* spp.), pile perch (*Rhacochilus vacca*), California sheephead (*Semicossyphus pulcher*), and cabezon (*Scorpaenicthys marmoratus*), were mainstays of human diets, along with smaller amounts of deeper water fishes such as swordfish (*Xiphias gladius*) and tunas (Scombridae).

Many intertidal and nearshore shellfish communities that were also important for human subsistence were common since the end of the Pleistocene, including California mussel (*Mytilus californianus*), red and black abalone (*Haliotis rufescens* and *H. cracherodii*), sea urchins (*Strongylocentrotus* spp.), and turban snails (*Chlorostoma* spp.).

During the Late Pleistocene, plant communities were also quite different on the islands, which today are home to numerous insular species not found on the mainland. Climatic conditions were cooler and wetter during the LGM, and pollen and other plant fossils of this age demonstrate that pines, cypress, and other conifers were more diverse and abundant than today.[11] Fossil cypress (*Cupressus* spp.) and Douglas fir (*Pseudotsuga menziesii*) logs, characteristic of modern conditions nearly 200 miles (~320 kilometers) or more to the north, found eroding from canyons on Santa Rosa and Santa Cruz islands have been dated to more than 17,000 years ago.[12] Near the end of the Pleistocene the conifer forests of Santarosae retreated significantly, with several species disappearing from the island, facilitating the expansion of oak woodland, chaparral, coastal scrub, and grassland/prairie habitats more characteristic of the Channel Islands today.

ENTERING THE AGE OF HUMANS (11,700 YEARS AGO TO TODAY)

The last glacial ended about 11,700 years ago, marking the close of the Pleistocene and the beginning of the Holocene. Not long ago, it seemed likely that the Holocene might be an interglacial period destined to be followed by yet another return to glacial conditions. With the steep rise in atmospheric carbon levels associated with the Industrial Revolution and our intensive use of fossil fuels, a return to glacial conditions now seems unlikely for the foreseeable future. With growing evidence that humans have extensively shaped and altered global landscapes and ecosystems—including those of the Channel Islands—some scientists have argued that the Holocene should be changed or merged with a new time period, the Anthropocene or Age of Humans.[13] Still hotly contested, a formal working group of the International Commission on Stratigraphy has proposed the Anthropocene as a new geologic epoch, with most participants arguing that it started recently, as little as 70 years ago. Regardless of terminology and timing of the Anthropocene, beginning more than 11,000 years ago humans became a driving force for ecological change on the Channel Islands.

As the Holocene dawned, humans had been on Santarosae for at least a thousand years. At this time, sea levels were roughly 200 feet (60–65 meters) lower than today, with as much as 40 percent of Santarosae's land area already lost to rising seas. The climate was also changing, from cool and wet to warmer and more arid conditions. The coniferous forests common during the last glacial were in retreat, with cypress and Douglas fir trees disappearing from the islands completely and pine forests, including Bishop pine (*Pinus muricata*) on Santa Cruz Island and Torrey pine (*Pinus torreyana*) on eastern Santa Rosa Island, retreating to the smaller refugia more typical of today. In contrast, kelp forests were more extensive near the beginning of the Holocene around Santarosae but gradually declined over time.[14] At least one productive estuary existed along the south-central coast of Santarosae but transitioned to marsh by about 6,000 years ago. While the productivity of terrestrial habitats was declining during the end of the Pleistocene and Early Holocene, the productivity of nearshore marine ecosystems may have increased.

Between about 11,000 and 9,000 years ago, Santarosae continued to shrink and fragmented into the four smaller islands of today.[15] The distance to the mainland, still just 6 miles (10 kilometers) or so at the beginning of the Holocene, continued to widen, gradually approaching the modern minimum distance of 12 miles (19 kilometers). With the Island Chumash and their ancestors on the islands continuously throughout the Holocene, anthropogenic alteration of island landscapes and ecosystems became apparent. Several animals were brought to the islands, either intentionally or by accident, including domesticated dogs (*Canis familiaris*), and perhaps the island fox (*Urocyon littoralis*), a small deer mouse (*Peromyscus maniculatus*), and the harvest mouse (*Reithrodontomys megalotis*) (see chapter 4). These biological introductions, along with the arrival of a top predator like humans, had significant effects on island landscapes and ecosystems. Some economically significant plants may also have been introduced to the islands or been moved between islands by the Chumash, including island scrub oaks.

These possible plant introductions and the animal introductions noted earlier are the subject of ongoing research to understand their origins and relationships to people. One of the most significant management techniques was regular burning of island landscapes by the Chumash, which helped preserve the grasslands rich in edible plant foods that provided a wealth of starchy roots, tubers, and corms.[16]

Beginning about 8,000 years ago rising seas and strong northeasterly winds caused the encroachment of extensive sand dunes on parts of the islands, especially on San Miguel and parts of Santa Rosa. Because these dunes consisted largely of calcareous sands, their presence altered vegetation communities, soils, and island hydrology. Since they were relatively well drained in the wet season, these dunes were attractive for human settlement, and large quantities of mussel, abalone, and other shellfish were collected, processed, and discarded by the Island Chumash and their ancestors on these landscapes. The weathering of calcareous sands and shells often led to root casts and caliche formations that were laid bare in historical times by massive erosion caused by heavy grazing from introduced sheep, cattle, and horses (figure 2.5). Severe erosion damaged many archaeological sites and exposed much older cemented dunes beneath the Holocene dune fields, attesting to

Figure 2.5. Fossil root casts and caliche formations of the caliche forest on San Miguel Island. *Source:* **open access image via islapedia.com.**

the long history of dune building on the islands. Fortunately, the end of ranching operations has been followed by the gradual recovery of island plant communities in many areas, along with ongoing soil and site stabilization.

SUMMARY AND CONCLUSIONS

The Northern Channel Islands, lying close to California's mainland coast but separated from it for millions of years, have a deep, unique, and dynamic geological and biological history. From their origins beneath the sea to their shaping by millions of years of tectonic and volcanic activity, climatic and sea level changes, marine erosion, and biological evolution, the islands have been in a constant state of flux. For at least 13,000 years, and possibly 18,000 years or more, humans have been a part of that story—adapting, innovating, and living with change. Significantly, the earliest human visitors—the Paleocoastal peoples discussed in the next chapter—occupied a much larger landscape, much of which is submerged beneath the waves today. At the moment, we know little about those portions of Santarosae that lie beneath the sea, but current research is shedding new light on their archaeological and paleontological potential.

In the chapters that follow, we explore many of those environmental and cultural changes, as well as the ingenuity and resilience of the Island Chumash and their ancestors. As we will see in chapter 3, the landscapes and productive marine resources of the Channel Islands and the larger Pacific Coast region—including vast kelp forests and other nearshore habitats that supported hundreds of species of shellfish, fish, marine mammals, and seabirds—attracted some of the First Americans, who may have followed a coastal "kelp highway" from northeast Asia into the brave new worlds of the vast Americas.

3

FIRST AMERICANS, FIRST ISLANDERS

Who were the First Americans, and where did they come from? When did they first arrive in the Americas, and how did they get here? We are in the midst of a "sea change" in understanding the answers to such questions, with new theories and exciting new tools to address them. For most of the 20th century, archaeologists believed the First Americans walked from Northeast Asia across the Bering Land Bridge (a vast area known as Beringia) near the end of the Pleistocene, passed through a narrow Ice-Free Corridor (IFC) as huge North American ice sheets melted, and rapidly spread across North America between about 13,500 and 13,200 years ago. Shortly after their arrival, they developed the iconic Clovis projectile point, large fluted points used for hunting large terrestrial mammals, which gives the archaeological culture its name. For decades, the Clovis-First model dominated scientific study of the First Americans. Most archaeologists assumed that occupation of the Pacific Coast occurred long after Clovis times and well after mammoths, mastodons, and other extinct Pleistocene mammals were hunted to extinction. In the last 10 years or so, our understanding of when the First Americans arrived and where they came from has changed significantly. California's Channel Islands have been instrumental in shaping current debates.

After more than a century of exploration and research, it is still not clear when humans first set foot on the Channel Islands or the broader California coast. In 1959, Phil Orr of the Santa Barbara Museum of Natural History found three human bones eroding out 37 feet (11 meters) below the surface near the mouth of Santa Rosa Island's Arlington Canyon. Arlington Springs Man, as these remains have come to be known, dates to nearly 13,000 years ago—contemporary with the famous Clovis hunting culture found nearly coast to coast in North America and once believed to be the first cultural group to discover the Americas. Two chert flakes and a bone bead found deep inside Daisy Cave on San Miguel Island may be even older, associated with burned soil and charred twigs dated to more than 18,000 years ago.[1] Claims for an even earlier human presence, championed by Orr for decades, were based on mammoth bones and fire features dated to more than 40,000 years ago. Orr's extraordinary claims have been dismissed by most scholars, but the islands may hold further surprises.

Currently, the earliest well-documented human presence on the Northern Channel Islands is dated to roughly 13,000 years ago. Clearly, the first humans to reach the islands did so in boats, as Santarosae has long been detached from the California mainland. The details of this voyage are shrouded in mystery; however, even the type of boats the first Islanders used is unknown as no archaeological evidence of such technology has been found. Nonetheless, in recent decades we have made tremendous progress in better understanding the lifeways of early Channel Islanders.

As we saw in chapter 2, the geography of the Channel Islands has changed dramatically through time, even during the past 15,000 to 20,000 years. Most challenging for archaeologists searching for the earliest signs of a human presence is the fact that roughly 70 to 75 percent of Santarosae has been drowned by rising seas since the end of the last glacial (see figure 2.2 in chapter 2). If early maritime peoples spent most of their time near the coast, the islands today are the tip of the proverbial iceberg, leaving us with the areas least likely to have been intensively used by seafaring peoples. Nevertheless, more than 100 Paleocoastal sites occupied between 13,000 to 8,000 years ago have been identified on the Northern Channel Islands, and more are found each year. Collectively, these sites are one of the most significant clusters of Paleoindian sites in the Americas. Few coastal areas in the Americas have the density of terminal Pleistocene and Early Holocene sites found on the Northern Channel Islands, making them one of the best places to understand the lifeways of some of the earliest people in the New World.

PALEOCOASTAL ORIGINS: THE KELP HIGHWAY HYPOTHESIS

Forty years ago Canadian archaeologist Knut Fladmark argued that the Pacific Coast offered a viable alternative to the Ice-Free Corridor route for the initial human colonization of the Americas.[2] At a time when Clovis was thought to represent the earliest human presence in North America, Fladmark was among the first to argue for a potential coastal dispersal of people into the Americas. The Coastal Migration Theory (CMT), which argued that groups of people followed Pacific Rim coastlines from Northeast Asia to the Americas near the end of the Pleistocene, was marginalized by most archaeologists for decades as a fanciful hypothesis with little tangible archaeological support.[3]

The major obstacle facing the CMT has always been the dearth of early coastal archaeological sites that would demonstrate that early migrants traveled along Pacific Rim coastlines. Such sites, however, are probably much harder to find than their terrestrial equivalents due to unique site preservation and discovery challenges. On a continental scale, the rise of post-glacial seas after about 18,000 years ago submerged nearly all of the Pacific Coast ancient shorelines early coastal peoples would have followed into the Americas. Assuming an ice-free coastal corridor opened in the North Pacific by about 17,000 years ago and sea levels stabilized about 7,000 years ago, 10,000 years of global sea level rise has resulted in the loss of approximately 10 million square kilometers of coastal plains from Beringia to southern Chile, with shoreline transgressions of less than 1 kilometers in some steep stretches of the Pacific Coast to approximately 500 kilometers in parts of Beringia.[4] Around the North Pacific Rim, the destructive effects of earthquakes, tsunamis, erosion, coastal development, and other destructive processes have also taken a heavy toll and made finding early coastal sites difficult.

Despite the early discovery and dating of the Arlington Springs Man remains, the Clovis-First model rendered the Channel Islands, California, and the Pacific Coast of North America peripheral to most discussions of the origins of the First Americans. Since the 1990s, however, growing evidence for late Pleistocene maritime voyaging to the islands of east Asia[5] and the broad acceptance of a pre-Clovis site dating at about 14,000 years ago at Monte Verde near the coast of central Chile[6] fueled a growing interest in the potential for a Pacific Coast entry into the Americas. The Monte Verde site, roughly 1,000 years older than Clovis and far to the south, included the remnants of a small wood structure that contained at least eight different types of seaweed.[7]

In 2007, a team of archaeologists and kelp forest biologists published a paper proposing the "Kelp Highway Hypothesis."[8] They hypothesized that nearshore North Pacific kelp forests—highly productive, entirely at sea level, and containing a diverse array of marine resources (shellfish, fish, marine mammals, seabirds, and seaweeds) that were similar from northern Japan to Baja California, Mexico—facilitated the dispersal of maritime peoples around the Pacific Rim near the end of the Pleistocene. Following interior routes from northeast Asia to South America at this time, in contrast, would have required crossing numerous geographic barriers (mountain ranges, large rivers, glaciers, deserts, etc.) and highly varied ecosystems with very different types of resources. A subsequent study documented hundreds of types of marine resources, either identical or very similar species, available along large stretches of the Pacific Coast. This would have allowed maritime people to utilize similar suites of resources as they spread around the Pacific Rim.[9] The coastal route contained numerous terrestrial resources as well, and many large Pacific Coast rivers, from the Yukon to the Sacramento, would have supported large and productive estuaries ideal for human settlement, as well as large runs of salmon and other anadromous fish that would have drawn coastal peoples deep into the interior of the Far West.

In recent years, the CMT and Kelp Highway Hypothesis have gone from marginal to mainstream, as a majority of archaeologists now believe that a coastal migration contributed to the initial peopling of the Americas. This paradigm shift places the Pacific Coast, California, and the Channel Islands squarely in the middle of debates about the peopling of the Americas.

CHANNEL ISLAND PALEOCOASTAL ARCHAEOLOGY

Despite the loss of nearly three-quarters of Santarosae's lowlands to rising seas, more than 100 Paleocoastal sites have been identified on the islands.[10] A few of these were initially identified by Phil Orr, who searched extensively for evidence of early human occupations on the islands, during the 1940s to 1960s.[11] Orr was fascinated by the origins of the first Islanders and was one of the first archaeologists to systematically use radiocarbon dating to understand the chronology of island cultures. Along with Arlington Springs, Orr described several Santa Rosa Island shell middens he believed to be late Pleistocene in age. In the late 1980s and early 1990s, Erlandson revisited most of these sites—dating them to no more than about 9,300 years ago—then began National Park Service–sponsored work at Daisy Cave on San Miguel, where a possible 11,700-year-old occupation had been identified below dense midden deposits dated between 10,000 and 8,500 years ago (sidebar 3.1).

Reconstructing Channel Island Shorelines by Leslie Reeder-Myers, Temple University

When people first arrived on the Northern Channel Islands, the world was a very different place. Glaciers covered large parts of the northern hemisphere, trapping much of Earth's water on land and causing sea levels to drop by as much as 120 meters. As the Pleistocene came to an end, glaciers melted, the runoff found its way to the oceans, and sea levels slowly rose, much like a bathtub filling with water. But unlike a bathtub's basin, the earth's crust is not stable—it constantly adjusts to the weight of ice or water or moves because of tectonics. When re-creating ancient shorelines, we must account for a complex variety of environmental factors, including variability in how water was distributed in the oceans, how Earth's crust has moved, and any sediment that has been deposited on top of—or eroded away from—Earth's surface.

Sophisticated computer mapping technology, called geographic information sciences, makes it possible to model all these different processes and generate high-resolution reconstructions of Santarosae and the Northern Channel Islands through time. We start with a bathymetric map, which shows the ocean floor as it is today. Then, we transform this map by raising or lowering different parts to reflect changes in Earth's crust and the thickness of sediment on top of the crust. Finally, we fill it back up with water, to the point where the ocean's surface was in the past. The result is a map that shows where shorelines were at that time.

Collectively, we have spent much of the past 30 years searching for additional Paleocoastal sites in the upland remnants of Santarosae. This search began with systematic surveys of ancient soils often buried beneath younger dunes or alluvium, focusing on geographic features that would have drawn coastal people into the interior of a relatively arid island: freshwater springs, caves and rock shelters, and outcrops of valued tool stone. These surveys were spectacularly successful, discovering and documenting scores of new Paleocoastal sites dating between about 12,200 and 8,000 years ago. Along the way, we added additional landforms to our search: blufftop locations providing panoramic views of ancient lowland or shoreline habitats and the locations of ancient wetlands that may have supported waterfowl and other resources. Recently, we also realized that upland grassland habitats were rich sources of edible roots, tubers, and corms from plants that drew coastal people to interior areas.[12]

During the past 20 years, as the number of early sites grew, we also learned to recognize distinctive Paleocoastal technologies, especially chipped-stone crescents and stemmed points known as Channel Island Amol (CIA) and Channel Island Barbed (CIB) points (figure 3.1). As discussed below, old museum collections contain scores of these artifact types, but their context, age, and significance were only recently recognized. Although more than 100 Channel Island crescents were known from old museum collections, the first island crescent from a known archaeological site—an approximately 9,000-year-old specimen from Daisy Cave—was only described in 2005. Since that time, numerous crescents have been documented from more than 25 island sites. A similar pattern holds true for CIA and CIB points, the age and distinctive characteristics of which have only been documented in the past decade or so.

Despite such progress, there is still much to be learned about the first Islanders. First, we are still missing a major component of the archaeological record—those sites located along ancient Santarosae shorelines and in coastal lowlands submerged by rising seas. Practically all the early sites we know of, therefore, represent just a small part of the story that illuminates what Paleocoastal people did while in the interior but not in the coastal settlements where they probably spent most of their time. Second, many of the known sites are "lithic scatters" that contain

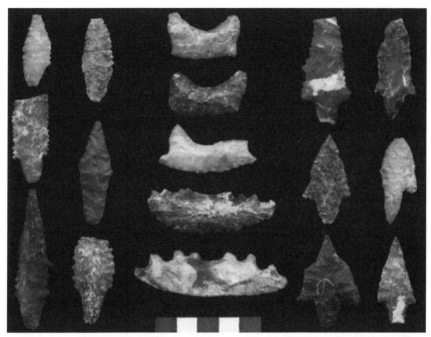

Figure 3.1. Paleocoastal chipped-stone tool technologies recovered from terminal Pleistocene sites on the Northern Channel Islands. First two columns: Channel Island Amol points; middle column: crescents or lunates; last two columns: Channel Island Barbed points. *Source:* **Jon M. Erlandson.**

only stone artifacts, and all organic remains have been lost to time and erosion. These can be rich sources of information about stone-tool technologies, but they tell us little about other aspects of Paleocoastal life. Third, even for those early sites that contain well-preserved animal and plant remains, few have been excavated, and many of these are short-term campsites that represent just small slices of time. Still, much progress has been made (sidebar 3.2).

Archaeology under the Waves by Amy Gusick, Natural History Museum of Los Angeles County

When Arlington Springs Man lived on Santarosae ~13,000 years ago, he and his kin occupied a very different landscape, one with bays, estuaries, and abundant food, raw material, and other resources that made the super-island an ideal home. Over generations, however, Santarosae underwent dramatic changes. As sea levels rose with the melting of glacial ice, nearly 75 percent of the island landmass was inundated, forever altering land and seascapes and sealing evidence of the earliest human occupations beneath 300 feet of ocean water.

Lost by rising seas were not only some of the oldest archaeological sites in the Americas, but also the landscape features and resources, such as paleochannels, tool stone resources, estuaries, bays, and tar seeps, critical for human survival. Finding and investigating these inundated features, places that would have attracted hunter-gatherers, may be our best chance to locate submerged terminal Pleistocene sites of Santarosae. The search for drowned Paleocoastal archaeological sites, however, presents daunting challenges. Have these features and sites been destroyed by wave and tidal energy? Where should we focus our search efforts on the more than 120 square miles (200 kilometers) of inundated Santarosae? Are these sites similar to those that we know from the terrestrial portion of the islands?

In the past 10 years, the first systematic efforts to address these questions and locate submerged archaeological sites of Santarosae have been undertaken. We are looking for answers by using marine mapping and seafloor coring technologies, such as ship-based sonar, electromagnetic surveys, and vibracore systems, that allow us to reconstruct and sample late Pleistocene submerged landscapes and environments. Through a multidisciplinary effort that includes archaeology, geology, biology,

Figure 3.2. Research crew launching geophysical survey equipment in order to map the seafloor and sub-seafloor stratigraphy along the Northern Channel Islands. Inset: Photograph of seafloor sediment cores collected along the Northern Channel Islands. *Source:* **Amy Gusick.**

geophysics, and tribal knowledge, we are collaborating and pooling knowledge to bring to life the drowned landscapes of Santarosae and target and
sample sections of the continental shelf that may have attracted Paleocoastal peoples. Finding an ancient archaeological site on the seafloor
is difficult and has yet to be realized, but every map we make and every
seafloor sample we collect allows us to better define the landscape and
environment of Santarosae and brings us one step closer to understanding
the place Arlington Springs Man called home (figure 3.2).

PALEOCOASTAL TECHNOLOGY AND INTERACTION

Nearly a century ago, an avid collector of Native American artifacts,
George Gustav Heye, whose collections became the foundation for
the National Museum of the American Indian in Washington, DC, and
New York, illustrated a beautiful projectile point found on San Miguel
Island during a 1919 expedition led by a notorious grave robber and
relic-hunter named Ralph Glidden. Heye described that point, with its
elaborate barbs and a needle-sharp point, as among the finest examples
of flint-knapping found anywhere in North America.[13] He also called it
"entirely too delicate" to have been used as an arrowhead, suggesting
that it was probably a ceremonial artifact. He may have been unaware
that similar points had been found by earlier antiquarians working on
the Northern Channel Islands, including specimens collected by Paul
Schumacher in the 1870s that ended up at the Smithsonian Institution. Until recently, these points, now known as CIBs and CIAs, were
assumed to be arrow points dating to the past 1,000 to 2,000 years. This
seemed a logical conclusion since bow-and-arrow technology is widely
believed to have spread across continental North America only in the
last few thousand years. However, archaeologists have recovered scores
of these point types in recent years from archaeological sites across the
Northern Channel Islands and demonstrated that they are Paleocoastal
in origin, dating between at least 12,200 and 8,000 years ago. It seems
most likely that these beautiful points were used to tip darts utilized in
hunting and fishing. Whatever their function, Heye was correct that
they were fashioned by extremely skilled flint-knappers, but he had no
way of knowing how old they were.

CIAs and CIBs are often found associated with crescents or lunates. These enigmatic artifacts are found in Paleoindian sites throughout the American Far West, part of a Western Stemmed Tradition that is as old or older than Clovis. They are nearly always found near lakes, marshes, estuaries, or other wetlands; additionally, they are widely believed to have served as transverse projectile points in the hunting of waterfowl and other birds.[14] They are abundant on the Northern Channel Islands but relatively rare on the southern islands, which are considerably more arid. At several sites on Santa Rosa Island, crescents have been found in buried soils accompanied by numerous bones of geese, ducks, and seabirds, including the earliest evidence for hunting the now extinct flightless scoter, *Chendytes lawi*.

Paleocoastal assemblages also include leaf-shaped bifaces and a variety of more expedient flake and core tools made from a variety of local rock types—scrapers, knives, choppers, and others made from cherts, igneous cobbles, and other materials. Although rare on the islands, occasional ground stone artifacts have been recovered from Paleocoastal sites, including a small pitted cobble—probably an anvil used to crack marine black turban snails—found at a 12,000-year-old shell midden rich in broken turban shells. At another 10,000-year-old shell midden on San Miguel, a fragment of a sandstone grinding slab was found that may have been used to grind plant foods or other materials. At several Paleocoastal island sites, iron-rich red ochre (hematite) has been found, a pigment, food preservative, and medicine used by early humans around the world. Red ochre also was dusted on shell beads buried with a human skeleton on Santa Rosa Island 9,500 years ago.

Shell beads have been recovered from several Paleocoastal sites dated between about 10,000 and 8,000 years ago. In every case so far, the beads were made from the shells of the purple olive snail (*Olivella biplicata*), from which the spire (top) was removed to allow for stringing (figure 3.3). As we shall see, the Island Chumash made many types of beads and ornaments (and other artifacts) from *Olivella*, abalone, and other marine shells for millennia, from Paleocoastal times to European contact and beyond.

Another raw material used by Paleocoastal people for a variety of tools was bone. Fragments of shaped bone tools have been found in an 11,700-year-old site on Santa Rosa Island, but they are too small

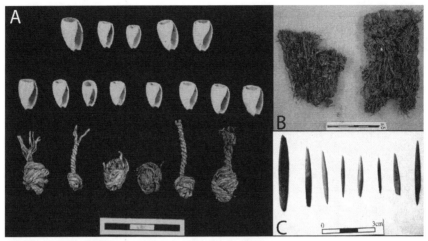

Figure 3.3. Paleocoastal technologies recovered from Daisy Cave and Cave of the Chimneys on San Miguel Island: (A) *Olivella* **shell beads and sea grass knots; (B) two fragments of sea grass sandals; and (C) bone gorges or bipoints, likely used as fishhooks.** *Source:* **Jon M. Erlandson.**

to determine their function. By at least 10,000 years ago, Paleocoastal peoples were making small, toothpick-like "bipoints" from bird and mammal bone. These bone gorges often have asphalt or scoring near their centers, leading most archaeologists to believe they were used as simple fishhooks. At Daisy Cave, where numerous gorges and more than 27,000 fish bones were recovered from Paleocoastal deposits dated between 10,000 and 8,500 years old, this interpretation seems particularly likely.[15] If so, the Paleocoastal bone gorges from the Northern Channel Islands are among the earliest fishhooks found in the Americas.

Finally, we know little about Paleocoastal technologies made from wood, plants, and other "perishable" materials that rarely preserve in archaeological sites, especially sites of great antiquity. We know boats were needed to colonize the islands and navigate the waters around them, for instance, but we can only guess what such boats were made of or looked like. From charcoal found in Paleocoastal sites, we know that a variety of local trees and shrubs provided fuels to cook with and stay warm. Aside from two rare exceptions, however, we know little about Paleocoastal clothing, houses, baskets, and other critical components of spears, darts, or tool handles typically made from wood or other plants. At Daisy Cave and Cave of the Chimneys on San Miguel Island, hundreds of pieces of woven sea grass (*Phyllospadix* spp.) were preserved in midden soils laced with salty seabird guano. These woven artifacts—mostly pieces of cordage used as string and possibly to make nets—are between 10,000 and 8,000 years old.[16] Fragments of two larger and more complex woven artifacts seem likely to have been parts of sea grass sandals.

PALEOCOASTAL SUBSISTENCE

Early evidence from Paleocoastal island sites suggested that shell-fish—especially mussels, abalones, limpets, and other rocky intertidal species—were one of the most important foods for early Channel Islanders, just as they were for contemporary peoples along the adjacent mainland coast.[17] At most Paleocoastal island sites, shellfish remains are, far and away, the most common refuse item. At first glance, it might seem the first Islanders were solely focused on intertidal shellfish that were abundant and easy to collect and process. Shellfish, however, are relatively poor sources of fat, carbohydrates, and calories, and it is difficult for people to survive on such foods alone. Most early sites along California's mainland coast contain numerous grinding stones that suggest a reliance on calorie- and carbohydrate-rich plant foods, a perfect nutritional complement to shellfish. The islands were thought to have few plant foods, in contrast, compared to the mainland, and until recently we had little evidence for their use by Paleocoastal peoples. There were hints of a broader Paleocoastal diet, however, especially at Daisy Cave on San Miguel Island, where Paleocoastal midden deposits produced marine mammal and bird bones, as well as scores of marine fish bones. A decade later, meticulous analysis of charred plant remains from the same strata at Daisy Cave identified small fragments of starchy bulbs, most likely from a family (Brodaeidae) of geophytes native to the islands.[18] Subsequent archaeological and botanical research—the latter informed by the recovery of native plant populations (especially the incredibly prolific blue dick, *Dichelostemma capitatum*)—has shown that these carbohydrate-rich corms and bulbs are and were relatively widespread and abundant on the islands.[19]

The discovery of two Paleocoastal sites on Santa Rosa Island dated to roughly 11,700 years ago further documented the diversity of Paleocoastal adaptations on the islands (figure 3.4). These sites, located not far from where Arlington Springs Man died a millennium or so earlier, are situated near the coast today but were inland sites some 4–6 kilometers from the coast when occupied.[20] At these buried sites, shellfish remains were relatively rare, but the bones of birds (especially geese and ducks), fish, and marine mammals were all relatively abundant. Recent analyses of proteins in fragmentary bones from these and other sites about 12,000 to 8,500 years old on Santa Rosa and San Miguel islands documented elephant seal, sea otter, and fur seal / California sea lion, suggesting even broader use of marine mammals.[21] Analyses of shellfish remains from a deposit dating about 11,000 years old on Santa

Figure 3.4. Photographs from CA-SRI-512, a terminal Pleistocene site near the mouth of Arlington Canyon that has produced a variety of Paleocoastal tools and faunal remains: (A) Erlandson assessing the site condition during its early discovery; (B) Rick excavating a unit at the sea cliff exposure; (C) archaeologists Tracy Garcia and Erlandson preparing an excavation unit; and (D) a bird bone and a stone tool eroding from the archaeological deposits. *Source:* Jon M. Erlandson and Torben C. Rick.

Rosa Island produced Venus clams (*Chione* spp.) and oysters (*Ostrea lurida*) from an ancient estuary, broadening the diverse array of foods collected by Paleocoastal peoples.

SOCIAL ORGANIZATION AND SEDENTISM

The limitations of the archaeological record, especially the lack of Paleocoastal sites located on older submerged coastlines, currently limits what we can say about the more social aspects of life for the first Islanders. The presence of beads and red ochre demonstrates an interest in art and ornamentation that served as markers of identity for our ancestors around the world. The incredible flint-knapping skill and artistry that went into making the often beautiful and symmetrical crescents and CIAs and CIBs surely blurs the lines between art and function in everyday life. With a wealth of food resources and raw materials locally available, there was probably little competition with neighboring groups for such resources and ample free time to experiment with new technologies and pursue aesthetics in daily life.

There were some resources available on the mainland that could not be found on the islands—deer and other terrestrial mammals among them—but these now seem to have been relatively few. Nonetheless, Paleocoastal peoples were clearly aware that there were neighboring people on the mainland and probably interacted with them more or less regularly. Importing and exporting materials, including some foods and value-added goods, probably occurred, but social contacts, alliances, marriage partners, and interactions may have been just as important. A small obsidian flake found in the 11,700-year-old site of CA-SRI-512 on Santa Rosa Island attests to such connections at a very early date. The tiny piece of obsidian, a natural glass traced to a volcanic flow in the Coso Ranges more than 180 miles (300 kilometers) into southern California's interior, demonstrates that Paleocoastal people were linked into broad interaction networks by at least the end of the Pleistocene, if not earlier.

One final aspect of interest is the evidence emerging that Paleocoastal people on the islands may have been relatively sedentary, often living in established villages for much of the year. Archaeologists, ourselves included, often consider Paleoindian and Paleocoastal people to have been relatively mobile. On islands where a wealth of resources are concentrated, and others can be harvested during daily foraging trips, however, why wouldn't people settle down in preferred locations? Certainly, the elaborate and diverse Paleocoastal technologies suggest the potential for sedentism, as do occasional human burials found in Paleocoastal sites. During excavation of the 11,700-year-old site of CA-SRI-512, interpreted as a seasonal winter camp focused on the hunting of migratory waterfowl, we uncovered the remnants of several postholes and two storage pits that may represent the remnants of a house or other structure. Recently, archaeologists have also analyzed oxygen isotopes preserved in the seasonal growth layers of marine shells to track ocean water temperatures and estimate what season of the year shellfish were collected. Application of this technique has tentatively identified year-round occupations of three Paleocoastal sites on San Miguel and Santa Rosa islands dated to about 10,000, 9,000, and 8,200 years ago. All of this suggests that Paleocoastal people lived on the islands permanently for several millennia and were at least semi-sedentary, occupying some favorable localities on the islands more or less year round.

CONCLUSIONS

Tremendous progress has been made in the past 25 years, but there is still much to learn about Paleocoastal peoples on the Northern Channel Islands. More than 100 sites occupied by these unique maritime people are now known for the islands; however, many more remain undocumented both on land and beneath the sea. Initial human settlement of the islands has been pushed back to at least 13,000 and perhaps more than 18,000 years ago. A diverse array of technologies has been documented: from sophisticated CIAs and CIBs, chipped-stone crescents, and leaf-shaped knives to cruder flake and core tools; bone bipoints and other artifacts; cordage, nets, and other basketry woven from sea grass; beads, red ochre, and asphaltum. From rare artifacts made from obsidian or other materials not locally available on the islands, we know the earliest Islanders also maintained social and economic connections with their mainland and interior neighbors. Paleocoastal peoples made and used boats for coastal travel and channel crossings and must have first colonized the islands with reliable watercraft. We currently don't know, however, what those boats were made of or what they looked like. What we do know is that early Islanders harvested a wide range of marine and terrestrial resources for millennia, including shellfish, fish, marine mammals, sea birds and waterfowl, as well as geophytes and other plant foods and fuels.

Although the islands appear to have been occupied by humans since at least Clovis times, it is intriguing that no diagnostic Clovis technologies, such as fluted projectile points, have been found among the thousands of stone tools recovered from Paleocoastal sites. Instead, an abundance of chipped-stone crescents and stemmed points seem to connect the first Islanders to the Western Stemmed Tradition of the American West, which has been linked to a potential coastal movement of maritime peoples around the Pacific Rim from Northeast Asia to the Americas. This "kelp highway" route may ultimately link the earliest Islanders to maritime Upper Paleolithic peoples who lived in northeast Asia 17,000 or more years ago, a hypothesis that has growing support from studies of human genomics, archaeology, geology, and biogeography.[22]

Only time will tell if this hypothesis is correct or if new evidence from the islands and surrounding areas will force yet another major shift in scientific thought. What we can be reasonably sure of is that important new evidence is likely to come from the submerged landscapes that surround the Channel Islands, where the earliest maritime peoples to settle the islands are likely to have spent most of their time. In the chapters that follow, we trace the descendants of Paleocoastal peoples on the islands through 8,000 years of continuous occupation by the Island Chumash and their amazingly resilient adaptations to an increasingly insular and ever-changing environment.

4

ISLANDS AND ISLANDERS IN TRANSITION

The first few millennia of human occupation of the Northern Channel Islands were an exciting time as Paleocoastal people colonized and explored new island land and seascapes. The islands were in a period of relatively rapid transition from before 13,000 years ago through about 7,500 years ago, when local sea levels were approaching modern levels and the islands were gradually assuming their present size and shape. Between 8,000 and 7,000 years ago, sea level rise was slowing, but the islands were still shrinking and becoming more isolated from each other and the mainland. Climate was also shifting into the warmer and dryer regimes of the Middle Holocene, extensive sand dunes were accumulating on San Miguel and parts of Santa Rosa Island, and kelp forest, rocky nearshore, and estuarine habitats were all in decline.

All these changes might have spelled doom for a people who had now lived on dramatically shrinking islands for several millennia, even as their populations had probably grown significantly. Instead, the ancestors of the Island Chumash appear to have been thriving in the Middle Holocene (~8,000 to 4,000 years ago), with the number of known sites growing substantially. Some of these sites contain a wealth of shellfish and other marine resources that reflect what some scholars have called a "marine cornucopia." New technologies appear while others disappear, new habitats are tapped, and new food sources became increasingly essential to Islander diets. Building on Early Holocene developments, Middle Holocene communities flourished despite tremendous ecological changes and challenges posed by sea level rise, regional warming, and dynamic shifts in ecological communities.

If the focus of the Paleocoastal period was human colonization of the islands and the lifeways of these early Islanders, the Middle Holocene is about how the descendants of these maritime pioneers developed into the complex and densely populated Island Chumash of historical times. This is an important question that sets the stage for a wide range of archaeological research. However, the Middle Holocene is often overshadowed by the bookends of the Paleocoastal period and the dramatic cultural developments and population growth that occurred during the last 4,000 years. Recognizing this research bias, Channel Island archaeologists have occasionally referred to the Middle Holocene as "the muddle in the middle," suggesting it was a relatively static and mundane time. This could not be further from the truth, as the Middle Holocene is a noteworthy period of cultural developments and environmental changes in its own right.

Between about 8,000 and 4,000 years ago, both the people and geography of the islands were in transition. Many of the most dramatic and important developments during the Middle Holocene relate to environmental changes, which coincide with important cultural change on the islands and elsewhere in southern California. The Middle Holocene likely marks the first time that dogs were brought to the Channel Islands. People may have also introduced gray foxes to the northern islands early in the Middle Holocene, which evolved into the iconic island fox and were transported to the Southern Channel Islands a few millennia later. The exploitation of plant foods probably intensified, as suggested by the first appearance of mortars and pestles and digging stick weights on the islands. People harvested a wide variety of shellfish, expanding on those species eaten by Paleocoastal peoples. Dense shell middens or pavements containing numerous large red abalone shells are a defining feature of the Middle Holocene, with interesting implications for kelp forests and environmental change. On Santa Rosa Island, the Abalone Rocks Estuary continued to be an important focus of sandy beach and estuarian subsistence activities, representing a divergence from the majority of sites that contain rocky intertidal species. At some Middle Holocene sites, people appear to have intensively hunted dolphins from boats as a coordinated nearshore hunting activity, a practice not seen with this intensity during any other time on the islands. These and other cultural developments form the backbone of this chapter, which demonstrates that the Middle Holocene was a dynamic interval—much more than just a bridge between Paleocoastal times and the rich and complex culture of the Island Chumash encountered by Spanish explorers almost 500 years ago.

MOBILITY, SEDENTISM, AND CHANGING TECHNOLOGIES

An interesting change occurred at the beginning of the Middle Holocene, approximately 8,000 years ago, with the disappearance of the finely made Channel Island Barbed points (CIBs) and crescents fashioned by Paleocoastal peoples. Instead, island people shifted away from delicate and finely made hunting technologies to more expedient chipped-stone tools. While many sites contain the remains of fishes, birds, and marine mammals, most Middle Holocene sites are overwhelmingly dominated by shellfish. This emphasis on expedient stone tools and shellfish is different from some aspects of the Paleocoastal period and has prompted researchers to speculate that a new group of people may have colonized the islands. This is controversial, but the change in some technologies—within the same group of people, an entirely new group, or an amalgamation of the two—is a defining feature of the Channel Island sites dated to 8,000 years ago and later. Significantly, other distinctive artifacts such as spire-removed *Olivella* beads and bone fishing gorges continue to be made and used across this transition.

Even as people relied more on expedient technologies and shellfish, however, there is an explosion of new artifact types made from bone, shell, ground stone, and other raw materials. In many ways, this is not surprising. These new technologies may simply represent processes of human adaptation, innovation, and landscape learning, as island populations grew and people made fuller use of all available habitats and materials. The changes in Middle Holocene technologies may also reflect changes in human settlement, mobility, and sedentism—the practice of increasingly living in one place.

Early to Middle Holocene changes in technology are evident at a large dune site found at CA-SRI-666 located on eastern Santa Rosa Island. CA-SRI-666 dates to around 8,200 years ago, an important time for understanding the transition from the Early to Middle Holocene and technological and subsistence shifts that took place as the Paleocoastal period came to a close. This site is positioned on an old dune ridge heavily affected by historical livestock grazing and wind erosion. Nearly all that remains from the archaeological site is found in a deflated lag deposit, meaning that just the stone tools and other heavy objects are left behind on the consolidated surface. Several small, cemented soil islands at the site are intact and contain shellfish, animal bone, and artifacts (figure 4.1). Because it has been largely deflated, CA-SRI-666 is like an open book, with hundreds of chipped-stone tools littered across the surface. We worked at the site in the 1990s and early 2000s, excavating a

Figure 4.1.   Photographs of several Middle Holocene sites on the Northern Channel Islands: (A) the cemented shell midden at CA-SRI-666 showing the thickness of the deposits; (B) Braje at the badly eroding red abalone midden, CA-SRI-26; (C) the dense 6,000-year-old red abalone midden at CA-SMI-481; and (D) sea cliff exposure of the red abalone midden, CA-SMI-388. *Source:* Torben C. Rick.

few small samples from the intact soil islands and systematically collecting chipped-stone tools. Analysis of 133 chipped artifacts confirmed that something different was happening at this site than in the Paleocoastal period. The finely made CIBs, Channel Island Amol points (CIAs), and crescents were gone, with only relatively simple bifacial points or knives, scrapers, and other expedient tools represented.[1]

Despite the relatively simple technologies found at CA-SRI-666, the archaeological materials from the soil islands revealed important trends in subsistence, including harvest of California mussels and estuarine shellfish. A few vertebrate remains were present, but perhaps most interesting was evidence for exploitation of blue dick corms, a starchy plant food used during the Paleocoastal period, for which evidence of human use seems to increase significantly in Middle and Late Holocene sites leading up to the Island Chumash at European contact. This diverse range of activities (plant harvest, estuarine and rocky shore shellfish, etc.), along with the size of the site and diversity of chipped-stone tools, led us to argue that CA-SRI-666 may have been a small village that people used as a residential base to access other temporary logistical sites. Despite the lack of more complex stone tools, the entire assemblage of materials found at the site suggests that a more complicated form of human settlement may have been emerging as the Middle Holocene dawned.

The general settlement pattern throughout much of the Middle Holocene is one of mobility, similar to the preceding Paleocoastal period. In this sense, relatively small groups of people were able to use large portions of the landscape, harvesting resources from new patches and productive habitats. Village formation and shifts to more sedentary lifestyles are important transitions that happen around the world, especially as people start practicing agriculture and need to stay in one location for longer periods to tend their crops. The Chumash are well known for having large villages or towns and being relatively sedentary when they were first contacted by Europeans, a topic we cover in the next chapter. CA-SRI-666 suggests that the growing shift from a relatively mobile to a more sedentary lifestyle may have begun during the Middle Holocene on the Northern Channel Islands.

University of California at Santa Barbara (UCSB) archaeologist Douglas Kennett, Jon Erlandson, and others conducted an interesting comparison of Middle Holocene settlements on the Northern and Southern Channel Islands, especially in relationship to climate change, such as warming and aridity during a period of global climate change known as the Holocene Climate Optimum or Altithermal. They found that the Southern Channel Island archaeological sites showed more evidence for early sedentism and house construction, while the over-all pattern on the northern islands showed continuity and continued mobility in the Middle Holocene. This may have been due to people in the more arid southern islands coalescing around favorable locations and freshwater sources. Despite this overall trend for Middle Holo-cene mobility, a few archaeological sites like CA-SRI-666 demonstrate increased sedentism on the northern islands by the Middle Holocene and deliberate settlement in productive locations. This pattern holds true at other resource-rich localities near Arlington and Tecolote can-yons on northwestern Santa Rosa Island, where we find evidence of increased sedentism during the earliest stages of the Middle Holocene.

From the 1940s to 1960s, Phil Orr worked extensively on northwest Santa Rosa Island, building a semi-permanent camp and living on the island for weeks or months at a time. As noted in chapter 3, he was very interested in the antiquity of human settlement, famously discovering the Arlington Springs Man remains. Orr was also interested in Middle and Late Holocene settlements and occasionally excavated house rem-nants; however, he was more focused on human burials. Typical of many archaeologists of his day, he concentrated on excavating cemeteries as a means to understand human cultural developments and to recover large quantities of well-preserved artifacts.[*]

Most of Orr's excavations were at Late Holocene cemeteries (see chapter 5), but he excavated burials at three adjacent Middle Holocene dune sites (CA-SRI-3, CA-SRI-4, and CA-SRI-5). At one site near Tecolote Point on the north coast of Santa Rosa Island, he excavated a cemetery in the 1950s containing 79 human burials, most of which appear to have been interred between about 7,600 and 7,400 years

[*] Such research is very rare today, and human cemeteries are protected by the Native American Graves Protection and Repatriation Act (NAGPRA), a 1990 federal law that protects Native Ameri-can burials from looting and scientific excavations and mandates that many culturally sensitive materials (human remains and funerary objects) be returned to Native American tribes. Archaeolo-gists today in California and beyond work closely with local tribes as partners and collaborators in all their research efforts and work together to preserve and protect archaeological sites.

ago. This cemetery is remarkable, in part, because it is emblematic of a large group living a relatively sedentary life in one of the island's most productive locations. Some of these burials contained shell beads, bone tools, and other offerings to the dead. The cemeteries on northwestern Santa Rosa Island, and others to the east at CA-SRI-41 that are between 4,000 and 3,000 years old, demonstrate a greater degree of sedentism at key locations during the Middle Holocene and prelude the large village complexes that occur on San Miguel, Santa Rosa, and Santa Cruz islands after about 2,000 years ago.

Similar perspectives are echoed at CA-SCRI-333 on western Santa Cruz Island. Here, evidence for numerous houses and a massive cemetery date from 6,000 to 2,000 years ago, or from the Middle to Late Holocene. UCSB archaeologist Lynn Gamble argues that this was a "persistent place," meaning that it was a focus of human settlement and other activities for millennia as people continually returned to construct houses, eat, celebrate, and perform rituals year after year.[2] Gamble suggests that the large site was intentionally created by people mounding sand, soil, and shell, deliberately transforming the landscape as a result of ceremony, feasting, and ritual.

Aspects of this settled life and reduced mobility are also present elsewhere on Santa Cruz Island. The Punta Arena site on the island's southwest coast, for instance, contains occupations dated from about 9,000 through 2,000 years ago. After about 7,000 years ago, a series of shell midden deposits contain a wide range of shellfish, fishes, birds, and marine mammals, such as dolphins (discussed more below). Like CA-SRI-666, these dense deposits support the idea that there was lower mobility at key locations in the Middle Holocene.

Still, other archaeological sites emphasize the mobile strategies and the diverse lifeways that may have been most common during the Middle Holocene. For instance, at Daisy Cave and Cave of the Chimneys, two adjacent caves on northeast San Miguel Island, there is nearly continuous evidence of Middle and Late Holocene occupation (following the Paleocoastal occupations at Daisy Cave described in chapter 3) from 8,000 years ago through about 2,000 years ago. These sites contain fairly transitory settlements, with occupations shifting back and forth between the two caves over the centuries. The caves also provide insights into the diversity of Middle Holocene technologies, including similar expedient stone tools like those identified at CA-SRI-666. Fortunately, the excellent preservation in both caves produced unique bone tools, including bird bone gorges that functioned as fishhooks, bone awls used for weaving or leather-work, *Olivella* spire-removed shell beads, and woven cordage made of sea grass. At Daisy Cave, sea grass artifacts date back to 10,000 years ago, and the tradition of these perishable technologies persists through the Middle Holocene, with sea grass cordage used for making bags, footwear, fishing nets, and other objects. Such technologies were likely made and used at many locations on the Channel Islands, but they rarely preserve in open-air archaeological sites.

Another technological hallmark that emphasizes the relationship between changing technologies, settlement and mobility, and the variability of Middle Holocene lifeways is the appearance of the mortar and pestle. Mortars and pestles first appear throughout much of California in the early part of the Middle Holocene. Many archaeologists speculate that they signify an intensification of acorn use, which may well be true in some areas, but the idea remains hotly contested. Oaks and acorns are relatively abundant on Santa Cruz and Santa Rosa islands today, but there is little direct evidence for acorn consumption by the Island Chumash and their ancestors—unlike much of mainland California. On the Channel Islands, it seems more likely that mortars and pestles served as a kind of ancient Cuisinart, used to process a variety of plant and animal foods. Large mortars and pestles are heavy and difficult to transport over long distances, and their presence in many Middle Holocene sites may support the idea that Islanders were becoming more sedentary and reliant on a wider range of plant and other foods to survive.

From the Middle Holocene to historical times, island archaeological sites often contain another unique ground-stone tool, perforated digging stick weights or donut stones (figure 4.2). These round stones, which look like donuts, were likely used as weights on the ends of digging sticks to assist in digging up root crops such as corms and tubers. Establishing the first appearance of such ground-stone artifacts can be difficult since many are found on eroded site surfaces and can't be effectively dated. However, like mortars and pestles, digging stick weights have clearly been found in some Middle Holocene shell middens on the Northern Channel Islands.

Figure 4.2. Photographs of Middle Holocene technology from the Northern Channel Islands: (A) a large red abalone shell and a marine mammal rib pry bar from the surface of CA-SMI-87 on San Miguel Island; (B) two donut stones (likely digging stick weights) from Santa Rosa Island; and (C) an asphaltum basketry impression (likely of a water bottle) from San Miguel Island. *Source:* **Torben C. Rick.**

Beads, particularly those made of shell, are a cultural hallmark of the Channel Islands since the Palecoastal period. Another Middle Holocene trend is an increase in the number of shell bead and ornament types, as people fashioned the materials around them into a greater diversity of personal objects of cultural significance. This includes a wider variety of *Olivella* shell bead types, including not only the spire-removed beads of the preceding Paleocoastal period but also new *Olivella* shell barrel, cap, and wall beads, which required more labor for the grinding of each bead. Tube-shaped purple scallop (*Hinnites multirugosis*) beads, which take advantage of a natural bright purple splotch of color near the hinge of the shell, also appear early in the Middle Holocene. Once thought to be very late signifiers of wealth and status, we now know these beads appear by the Middle Holocene, nearly 8,000 years ago. Finally, beads made from giant keyhole limpets, as well as the shiny interior mother of pearl from abalones, are relatively common, particularly as burial offerings, in the Middle Holocene.

Collectively, these patterns illustrate the importance of the Middle Holocene as a time of transition and expansion and demonstrate the relationships between changes in human settlement, cultural developments, and technology. There is increasing evidence for the beginnings of settled village life at some central locations in the Middle Holocene, although many people continue to be fairly mobile. Similarly, there is a shift toward the use of more expedient chipped-stone technologies and, at the same time, an explosion in shell, bone, and ground stone technologies, as well as the earliest known appearance of woven water bottles sealed with asphaltum. In much the same way, human diets during the Middle Holocene expanded to take full advantage of a wider range of available resources. All this suggests that the Middle Holocene was a period of transition that sets the stage for even more dramatic cultural developments of the last 2,500 to 3,000 years.

RED ABALONES, SEA OTTERS, AND KELP FORESTS

The California Coast is famous for its rich and productive kelp forests. Much like temperate forests on land, kelp forests support an incredible diversity of plants and animals, including seals and sea lions, fishes, abalones and sea urchins, sea otters, and much more. Kelp forests provided food and other resources for the people who lived on the Channel Islands since initial colonization and were a focus of subsistence activities until historical times. Despite the diversity and importance of kelp forests for hundreds of species, their basic function and structure is regulated by physical factors (sunlight, water clarity, and rocky substrates) and a few keystone animal predators, from humans and sea otters, to sea urchins, California spiny lobsters, and California sheephead. In recent years, archaeologists have used data from Channel Island archaeological sites to understand the importance and abundance of many of these organisms and, ultimately, how humans and environmental change may have shaped California coastal and intertidal ecosystems. Paleocoastal sites contribute to these reconstructions, but the full picture of past human influence on Channel Island environments becomes apparent in the Middle Holocene.

Scattered around San Miguel, Santa Rosa, and western Santa Cruz islands, as well as San Nicolas Island and parts of the central California mainland, are a unique and mostly Middle Holocene site type called red abalone middens. These sites often occur as large, conspicuous pavements of large red abalone and other shells. Most are lenses of dense shell midden roughly 20–40 centimeters thick, and many are encased in dune sands. When excavated and analyzed, archaeologists have determined that shellfish assemblages from such sites can contain 90 percent or more red abalone shell, but some red abalone middens contain as little as 5 percent red abalone. Many also contain abalone pry bars, bone tools usually made from marine mammal ribs that are shaped like a flat crowbar used to pry abalones from rocks. People harvested red abalones on the islands for at least 12,000 years, but most red abalone middens date between 8,000 and 3,000 years ago, with an even narrower range in the warmer waters of Santa Cruz Island.

Archaeologists have been interested in understanding the timing and distribution of red abalone middens since the 1950s when Carl Hubbs, a biologist and naturalist from the University of California at San Diego, explored the links among red abalone middens, human behavior, and climate. Hubbs noted that red abalones prefer cooler water temperatures and are usually found in deeper subtidal waters of south-central California and the Northern Channel Islands. In contrast, warmer water–loving black abalones are mostly intertidal in this region and would have been much easier for Indigenous people to harvest. In essence, people were either diving for red abalones in deeper, cold waters, or changes in sea surface temperature, such as localized oceanic cooling, allowed red abalones to expand into the intertidal as they do in northern California today. UCSB archaeologist Mike Glassow spent much of his career exploring red abalone middens, testing and expanding on Hubbs's work. Glassow and his colleagues excavated several red abalone middens on Santa Cruz Island and analyzed stable isotope in shells from the middens; the team argues that the sea surface temperature model best explained the appearance of red abalone middens.[3]

On Santa Cruz, most red abalone middens occur between about 6,200 and 5,800 years ago, when proxy indicators from Santa Barbara Basin cores suggest that marine waters were cooler. However, much of the Middle Holocene on either end of this brief cool period was characterized by warmer sea surface temperatures, which would have restricted the movement of red abalones into the intertidal.[4] Combining data from red abalone middens from Santa Cruz, Santa Rosa, and San Miguel islands, we found that marine cooling may have affected the appearance of red abalone middens on Santa Cruz, but on Santa Rosa and, particularly, San Miguel islands, whose waters are naturally cooler than Santa Cruz due to stronger upwelling, cooling marine temperatures had little or no effect on red abalone harvest.[5] On Santa Cruz, red abalone middens are restricted to cool water intervals, but on San Miguel and Santa Rosa they span both warm and cold intervals for roughly 5,000 years. Even today on western San Miguel Island, red abalones can sometimes be found in rocky intertidal zones.

Were people diving for red abalones in the past? This simple question is difficult to answer. On the Northern Channel Islands, particularly on the western islands, nearshore waters are relatively cold, rough, and turbid because they experience considerable wave action. Imagine diving in these waters without a mask, snorkel, wetsuit, or other modern amenities. Despite these challenges, people almost certainly did some free diving in the distant past on the Channel Islands to harvest red abalones and other subtidal foods.

A recent study by Eastern New Mexico University bioarchaeologist Susan Kuzminsky and her colleagues investigated the possibility that some human skeletons from the Northern Channel Islands contain evidence for diving in cold waters, especially during the Middle Holocene.[6] Kuzminsky examined human skulls for evidence of "swimmer's ear"—also known as the tongue-twisting medical label "external exostosis of the auditory meatus"—a condition where bone starts to grow over the auditory meatus (ear canal) as a response to repeated diving, surfing, or swimming in cold water. Kuzminsky found that some Channel Island skeletons contain this condition, supporting cold water diving, but there was no evidence that it was more common during the Middle Holocene's red abalone midden period. We suspect people were diving and wading in relatively shallow waters to obtain red abalone and other resources, but it is hard to say precisely how much, where, or when.

Red, black, and other abalone species were once an important commercial fishery in California, with massive landings from San Miguel and other Channel Islands. For the last decade or so, we have worked to understand how archaeological records from Channel Island red abalone middens and other sites might help us understand modern conservation and sustainability of these foods, as well as the broader health of kelp forest ecosystems. From marine ecologists and fisheries biologists, we learned that middens containing hundreds or thousands of large red abalone shells could not occur if sea otters were abundant in local waters. Sea otters eat copious numbers of red abalones and, in a healthy kelp forest, force red abalones to live in inaccessible rocky cracks where they are protected from otters but can feed on drift kelp. Sea urchins, another prized food for sea otters, also feed on kelp and should be relegated to cracks where otters regularly feed. Modern fisheries data confirm that productive abalone and urchin fisheries are not sustainable where sea otters are abundant. If red abalone middens indicate that sea otters were scarce or absent in Channel Island waters during the Middle Holocene, what does this mean about ancient kelp forests and the role of people in shaping their productivity?

In the 1970s, research in the Aleutian Islands demonstrated that removing sea otters from Alaskan kelp forests could result in the hyperabundance of urchins and produce what are called "kelp barrens," areas with no kelp that are much less productive than healthy kelp forests.[7] Freed from predation, urchins rapidly multiply and expand out from their cracks and crevices to feed directly on kelp. In short order, such urchin blooms can clear cut a highly productive kelp forest ecosystem.

Southern California kelp forests are older and more complicated than those in the far North Pacific. Here, California sheephead (a kelp forest fish), spiny lobsters, and sunflower sea stars are also voracious predators of urchins and help regulate kelp forest health. If urchins become hyperabundant, they are preyed upon and regulated by a variety of sea creatures, not just sea otters. Despite this diversity, smaller kelp barrens do occur in California waters, especially where some of these other predators are heavily fished. These complex ecological relationships hint at a picture of red abalone middens, and perhaps other Channel Island site types, suggesting that they result from processes far more complicated than variations in sea surface temperature across space and time. Did humans, as one of the apex predators in nearshore waters of the ancient Channel Islands, influence the abundance of sea otters, red abalone, sea urchins, sheephead, and even kelp forests themselves? The answer to this question is yes, but it is complicated.

Analysis of the abundance of sea otter bones in San Miguel Island middens shows that they were hunted, likely for their warm pelts and meat, since Paleocoastal times. Comparing the density of sea otter bones to those of sea urchin remains, however, suggests that there were times in the deep human history of the Channel Islands when short-lived kelp barrens formed—times when humans appear to have reduced otter populations, allowing sea urchins to multiply and create localized kelp barrens.[8] Chumash foragers responded by increasing their predation on urchins, creating dense lenses of urchin tests and spines in numerous Middle Holocene middens, which may have helped kelp forests to regenerate. Altogether, such patterns suggest that Channel Islanders influenced the structure and function of kelp forest ecosystems on the Channel Islands during the Middle Holocene.

Caution requires us to note that the data used to support this scenario are preliminary or need more testing. Perhaps people weren't overhunting or actively managing otter populations, but they restricted sea otter access to local catchments through their persistent presence. If people were foraging in local kelp forests every day, they may well have been a deterrent for otters, who might flee to places where people were less frequent visitors. Another complex factor in this argument is the other three primary predators of urchins: California sheephead, California spiny lobsters, and sunflower sea stars. Sunflower sea stars are common intertidal and kelp forest predators; however, they are an unlikely food source for humans, and their skeletons leave little that would preserve in archaeological sites. Crab remains are common in Channel Island middens, but spiny lobster remains are rarely identified. Consequently, we haven't yet been able to account for sea star or lobster abundance in our models. California sheephead, however, were an important prey item for people on the Northern Channel Islands for 10,000 years or more. Nonetheless, there are no clear indications, as of yet, that ancient Islanders influenced the abundance of sheephead.

Ultimately, the story of red abalones, sea otters, kelp forests, and humans is complex. In many ways, the dynamics of these ecosystems demonstrate that since at least the Middle Holocene, and likely earlier, humans were a keystone predator in nearshore Channel Island marine ecosystems and influenced their structure and function for millennia. Human influence on Channel Island environments often worked in tandem with natural climatic and environmental change, such as Holocene sea level rise, fluctuating sea surface temperatures, drought, and many other variables.

ESTUARIES, SANDY BEACHES, AND DOLPHINS

Red abalone middens and kelp forests are an important part of the Middle Holocene, but they are one component of a larger story of islands and Islanders in transition. We have seen how human technologies changed during the Middle Holocene and how people continued to have relatively mobile settlement strategies, but large sites and cemeteries at prominent locations provide snapshots of increasing sedentism. Further evidence for this diversity of human lifeways and environmental change comes from excavations of shell middens from other site types, particularly those that are not red abalone middens. These include the appearance and decline of an estuary on Santa Rosa Island, Pismo clam middens that suggest greater use of sandy beaches, and evidence for dolphin hunting that indicates a focus on larger, deep water resources.

As noted in chapter 3, Paleocoastal people lived in a rapidly changing geography marked by shrinking island landscapes. Rapid sea level rise can also create estuaries at the mouths of coastal canyons. Estuaries form where freshwater and ocean water mix, creating some of the richest ecosystems on Earth. Productive estuaries formed at the end of the Pleistocene up and down the Pacific Coast as rising seas flooded canyon mouths and created protected embayments ideal for ancient maritime peoples. Numerous paleoestuaries formed along the Santa Barbara mainland coast and were magnets for early human settlement until sea level rise slowed roughly 6,000 years ago and many smaller estuaries filled with sediment and disappeared.[9] Only the largest of these estuaries persisted into historical times, such as the Goleta Slough and Carpinteria Slough.

On the Channel Islands, no productive estuaries exist today, and until about 25 years ago, it appeared that none did since humans first colonized the islands. Research on eastern Santa Rosa and western Santa Cruz, however, has shown that at least one estuary existed in this area in the past. This includes archaeological evidence of estuarine shellfish exploitation in the Crescent Bay area since at least 11,500 years ago (see chapter 3). Paleocoastal peoples clearly harvested estuarine and marsh resources, but the best evidence for human harvest of estuarine shellfish on the Northern Channel Islands comes from the Abalone Rocks Paleoestuary (now a marsh) near Old Ranch Canyon on eastern Santa Rosa Island. In this area, more than a dozen archaeological sites attest to the use of estuarine shellfish like Venus clams, oysters, and Washington clams between about 8,000 and 5,000 years ago. Most of these middens are dominated by mussels and other rocky intertidal shellfish, with estuarine shell making up 20 percent or less, an important supplementary part of the diet. Like many Middle Holocene sites, vertebrate remains are rare, and there is no evidence that people intensively harvested aquatic birds or sharks or shallow water fishes that congregate in estuaries. Nonetheless, the Abalone Rocks estuary adds to the story of Middle Holocene transition and diversity, showing how people opportunistically responded to landscape change on century to millennial scales.

The vast majority of shellfish remains found in California Island sites throughout the Holocene are from rocky intertidal habitats and are dominated by California mussels and, sometimes, red and black abalones. Other rocky shore species such as turban snails and limpets are abundant at certain specialized sites. Like the Abalone Rocks estuary, however, a relatively small percentage of sites—dating primarily to the Middle Holocene—contain the shells of Pismo clams, found in surf-swept sandy beaches. On eastern Santa Rosa Island, for instance, CA-SRI-209 contains two small midden mounds, which date between about 4,700 and 4,300 years ago and contain 90 percent Pismo clam. Similar middens date to the Late Holocene (most around 1,000 years old) on western Santa Cruz Island and one (CA-SMI-181) on San Miguel Island contains numerous Pismo clam shells dated to about 7,000 years ago. Like red abalones, sea otters are voracious predators of Pismo clams. Although only a few such site types have been identified on the Channel Islands, Pismo clam middens highlight the diversity of shellfish exploitation by Channel Islanders during the Middle Holocene and support the idea that sea otters were rare or absent in many Northern Channel Island habitats.

We have discussed sea otters, sheephead, and other vertebrates, but most of our discussion for the Middle Holocene has focused on shellfish remains. A major exception, and one of the more interesting Middle Holocene patterns, is evidence for relatively intensive dolphin hunting. Like the harvest of Pismo clams and estuarine shellfish, dolphin hunting was likely a Middle Holocene hunting strategy practiced at key locations, such as Punta Arena on southwest Santa Cruz Island and Eel Point on western San Clemente Island. Some scholars have suggested that beached dolphins may have been scavenged from the shore, but substantial evidence points to boat-based hunting or herding and a hunting strategy uniquely adapted to the local geography. Questions may persist about the nature of Middle Holocene dolphin hunting, but their harvest in relatively large numbers in such locations adds to the diversity and sophistication of subsistence strategies on the Channel Islands at this time (sidebar 4.1).

Channel Island Dolphin Hunters by Michael A. Glassow, University of California, Santa Barbara

On the south coast of Santa Cruz Island, archaeological excavations in 1997 revealed that deposits dating between 6,300 and 5,300 years ago contain unusually large numbers of dolphin bones (figure 4.3). This massive archaeological site, known as the Punta Arena site, was occupied for more than 6,000 years, and it is only during this brief interval where we see the intensified hunting of dolphins. In fact, deposits dating both earlier and later lack significant densities of dolphin bone, as does almost any archaeological site of any age across the Northern Channel Islands. The Middle Holocene dolphin hunters at Punta Arena captured four species of dolphins, Risso's dolphin, Pacific white-sided dolphin, common dolphin, and northern right whale dolphin. These species still swim in waters around the island today.

Why are dolphin bones so abundant at this site compared to others on the island? The presence of a deep, steep-sided submarine canyon about 2 kilometers offshore appears to be the principal factor. Upwelling of sea water occurs adjacent to this canyon, which results in high productivity of a variety of marine organisms such as small schooling fish and squids upon which dolphins feed. When dolphins congregated at this location, hunters could be assured of success. Nowhere else around the island would

Figure 4.3. Photograph of *in situ* dolphin vertebrae exposed along the wall of a gully that bisects the shell midden deposits at the Punta Arena site on Santa Cruz Island. *Source:* Michael A. Glassow.

dolphins gather in such large numbers so close to shore. Supporting this hypothesis is the discovery of an archaeological site on Santa Catalina Island and another on San Clemente Island, both in the southern group of the Channel Islands, that contain large quantities of dolphin bones and are adjacent to submarine canyons. Cooler ocean water temperatures during this period may also have fostered higher marine productivity, and dolphins may have been especially abundant near the submarine canyon during this interval.

Beyond dolphin and sea otter hunting, evidence for Middle Holocene hunting of seals and sea lions is limited, although people did hunt or scavenge California sea lions, fur seals, and, at times, harbor and elephant seals. Ultimately, the evidence for dolphin hunting and harvest of seals and sea lions adds to a growing body of evidence for the opportunistic nature of Middle Holocene environmental interactions, building on patterns from the Paleocoastal period. This adaptive flexibility and experimentation gave rise to the full cultural florescence of the Island Chumash after about 3,000 to 2,000 years ago in the Late Holocene.

TRANSFORMING ISLAND LANDSCAPES

The Middle Holocene is the first time that we can observe in detail how people influenced island ecosystems and how natural climatic changes affected these environments and the people who depended on them. We have described some of the ways people influenced island seascapes, but people also actively shaped island terrestrial ecosystems. This is particularly evident in human use of fire, the use and management of some terrestrial plants, and deliberate human introduction of some mammals and plants to the islands. Many of these changes were set in motion during the Paleocoastal period but develop in the Middle Holocene and then explode after about 3,000 years ago.

Fire is an Indigenous management tool used around the world and covered in detail in chapter 5. Wildfires have been an important component of Channel Island and broader California ecosystems for millennia. The Chumash are known to have burned mainland landscapes in historical times. Middle Holocene, and perhaps earlier, people likely did so on the Channel Islands as well. University of California at Davis geologist Nicholas Pinter and colleagues have suggested that ancient Channel Islanders set extensive fires since initial colonization, while Kennett and others argue that these were wildfires, perhaps triggered by a comet or other extraterrestrial impact.

Northern Arizona University paleoecologist Scott Anderson and colleagues provided a detailed record of fire history for eastern Santa Rosa Island based on a 7,000-year charcoal record from the Abalone Rocks Estuary/Marsh.[10] This record contains evidence for a spike in fires around 4,000 years ago; something they attribute to human-set fires. The spike was not consistent with any previous patterning, and the sheer abundance of charcoal suggests human, rather than natural, ignition. By at least the end of the Middle Holocene (and probably much earlier) and through historical times, fire record histories suggest that the Island Chumash used landscape burning as a management tool—a topic we return to in the next chapter and an important area for future research.

Plants were a crucial source of food and resources for people, with Paleocoastal peoples known to exploit corms and other plant foods. Harvest of corms increased in the Middle Holocene, and people gathered a wide variety of other plant resources on the islands, including lemonade

berry, chia seeds, and acorns, although we know very little about the
scale of harvest. Fire, then, was likely used to create and maintain open
grassland habitat and enhance ecosystems where economically important plant resources thrived. These activities likely intensified in the
Late Holocene, but their foundations date back to at least the Middle
Holocene.

Middle Holocene Islanders further transformed landscapes by introducing or moving mammals, plants, and, perhaps, other organisms
(insects, amphibians/reptiles, etc.) from the mainland to the islands.
Called translocations, the introduction of new organisms by people to
islands and new habitats is something people have been doing for tens of
thousands of years, including movement and introduction of both wild
and domesticated species. In fact, many of the ecological challenges
we face today with invasive species around the world are the product
of modern or historical translocations. To better understand ancient
Channel Island translocations, new research is using stable isotopes and
ancient DNA to track introductions (sidebar 4.2).

**Biological Introductions and Archaeogenetics by Courtney A. Hofman,
University of Oklahoma**

One of the fascinating questions about Channel Island environments is
this: How and when did the animals we see today on the islands first
arrive? In some cases, such as with mammoths that once roamed the
northern islands, animals swam across the Santa Barbara Channel during
cold glacial intervals, when water gaps were significantly smaller. However, many animals are poor long-distance swimmers. Other possibilities
include rafting, when a pregnant female floats to the island on debris, or
introduction by people as they traveled from the mainland to the islands.
Distinguishing between these three scenarios is challenging and requires
interdisciplinary methods that draw on paleontology, archaeology, and
genetics.

The study of ancient DNA (paleogenomics) allows us to compare past
populations to modern ones and establish evolutionary relationships.
Using a specialized laboratory that minimizes the risk of contamination,
DNA is extracted from animal bones recovered from island and mainland archaeological sites (figure 4.4). After careful sequencing, specialists look for similarities and differences between samples within each
island, across islands, and with the mainland. If very few differences are
found between samples from a single island, the animal likely arrived via

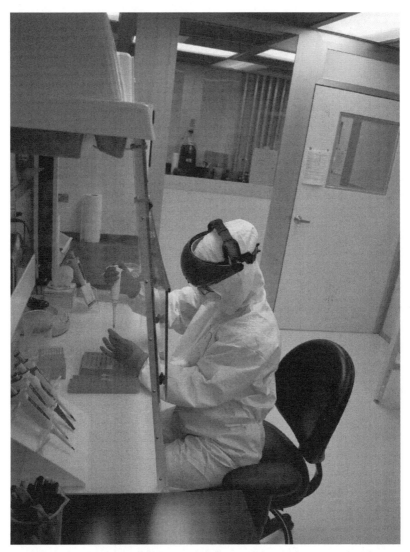

Figure 4.4. Ancient DNA researcher with anti-contamination protocols in place conducting experiments at the Laboratories of Molecular Anthropology and Microbiome Research at the University of Oklahoma. *Source:* Courtney A. Hofman.

rafting or swimming. If significant differences are identified, there likely were multiple introductions, suggesting humans repeatedly transported mainland animals to the island. To determine if this was an intentional or unintentional introduction, genetic data is combined with radiocarbon dates to establish the timing of arrival. A variety of other information sources, such as isotopic data to reconstruct the animal's diet, natural history information about the animal's biology, and ethnographic data about the animal's relationship with humans, all become critical to further explore the "when" and "how" of the animal's island origins. These techniques are increasingly being used to understand potential island fox, deer mouse, and plant (e.g., oaks) introductions to the Channel Islands or between islands.

Determining whether humans introduced an organism or if it was transported naturally by a drift log (animal or plant), bird (seeds), or other means is challenging. The list of taxa that could have been first introduced by people to the Channel Islands is growing, with island deer mice likely introduced by people to Santarosae more than 10,000 years ago as accidental stowaways on boats. Based on genetic data, gray foxes appear to have been introduced to the Channel Islands sometime before 9,000 years ago, with the earliest archaeological island fox specimens radiocarbon dated to about 7,300 years ago. Sometime after their arrival, island foxes were transported from the Northern to Southern Channel Islands, with genetic data suggesting this occurred around 7,000 years ago and the oldest archaeological specimens radiocarbon dated to around 5,900 years ago.

One organism that was undeniably introduced by people is domesticated dogs. We investigated the evidence for the initial appearance of dogs on the Channel Islands, noting that their remains have been found on all but the smallest islands of Anacapa on the northern island chain and Santa Barbara in the southern chain.[11] Based on careful radiocarbon dating of their skeletal remains from island archaeological sites, dogs were transported to the Northern Channel Islands by humans at least 6,000 years ago. While these remains are not necessarily the earliest dogs on the Channel Islands and future research may produce even earlier dates, they are the minimum age of first introduction and demonstrate that, by at least the Middle Holocene, people were purposefully moving animals from the mainland to the islands in boats.

A few studies of stable isotopes on both island foxes and dogs document the commensal relationship between these animals. Most dogs seem to be nearly identical to humans in their isotopic signature, meaning that they were consuming similar amounts of marine protein and being provisioned by people. Most ancient island fox bones, however, have the same isotope profile as modern island foxes, suggesting they were eating more terrestrial foods, like mice, insects, and fruits. One reason people might have introduced foxes was to help control mice populations, which had few island predators except for barn owls and dogs. In this scenario, the disparity between what dogs and humans versus foxes were eating makes sense. In addition to controlling mice, foxes could have been introduced to the islands for their pelts, as they appear on the islands when sea otters seemingly were declining. We know from ethnographic accounts, and evidenced by the historical fur trade for sea otter pelts (see chapter 6), that warm, fur-lined clothing was highly valued on the often cold and foggy Northern Channel Islands. Island fox pelts would have made an excellent substitute if otters were in short supply. In addition to these mammals, some researchers have suggested that island oaks were being moved between islands by Native Americans. The transportation of other economically valued plants is a distinct possibility and an area in need of more interdisciplinary research. The study of evidence for Middle Holocene use of fire, plant management, and species introductions is just beginning, but exciting research points to the time period between 8,000 and 4,000 years ago as a key interval of island transformations, when nearshore marine and terrestrial ecosystems were increasingly influenced by human activities.

CONCLUSIONS

From the formation of red abalone middens to an increase in the production of beads and mortars and pestles, as well as the introduction of dogs and foxes, the Middle Holocene was an important period of transition on the Channel Islands. Many developments between 8,000 and 4,000 years ago illustrate both the effects of natural environmental change and the growing influence of people as landscape engineers and keystone island predators. The appearance and subsequent disappearance of the Abalone Rocks estuary is a classic example of natural environmental change, while the translocation of dogs and foxes and anthropogenic burning is an indication of deliberate human transformation. The trends and transitions of the Middle Holocene demonstrate that, far from being a lackluster "muddle in the middle," this period played a central role in the cultural and environmental history of the Northern Channel Islands. Many patterns observed in Paleocoastal times continue, but Islander lifeways were clearly in transition, with permanently occupied villages and cemeteries at key locations, an expansion of diets, and the use of new habitats and resources. The Middle Holocene was the critical bridge to the amazing cultural, technological, and artistic complexity of the Late Holocene, for which the Island Chumash are known worldwide.

5

THE ISLAND CHUMASH

Not long ago the Northern Channel Islands were very different than the remote, largely empty, and wild places they seem today. As recently as the early 19th century, the archipelago was a bustling population center, teaming with Chumash villages, hunting and fishing camps, stone-tool quarries, and much more, many found in places that had been occupied or visited for millennia. Roughly 3,000 people lived on the Northern Channel Islands in the 18th to early 19th centuries. The Island Chumash occupied thriving villages of multiple families with some of the largest containing more than 100 people.

People spoke several distinct dialects of the Chumashan language family, and Chumash villages and towns dotted the mainland coast from Malibu to San Luis Obispo County, the adjacent mountains and valleys, and the Northern Channel Islands. Along the mainland coast, around the margins of the large Goleta estuary, some Chumash towns contained as many as 1,500 people.[1] Similar to modern cities and towns, the people who lived at these villages represented a wide cross-section of Chumash society, including village chiefs, craft specialists, religious and ceremonial leaders, laborers, fishers, elders, children, and myriad other members of the diverse fabric of Chumash society. A typical village at one of the prominent Channel Island drainages today, like Prisoners Harbor, Scorpion Anchorage, or Bechers Bay, contained 10 to 25 houses or more, with 10 or more people to each home. Dogs were common pets at many of these villages. Communal spaces for interaction, ceremonies, dances, exchange, and subsistence were present, and most villages were flanked by cemeteries. Sophisticated boats known as *tomols*—made of split redwood planks sewn together and caulked with tar and pine pitch—lined the beaches when not in use. In short, Island Chumash settlements were vibrant communities of individuals, interacting with each other, neighbors near and far, and local environments.

We know a great deal about the Chumash during historical times thanks to rich ethnohistoric accounts that describe villages, technologies, subsistence practices, social organization, cosmology, and much more. These include direct accounts from the late 18th and early 19th centuries recorded by John P. Harrington, Henry W. Henshaw, and other early anthropologists. Four Chumash community members, Fernando Librado Kitsepawit, Luisa Ygnacio, María Solares, and Juan Estevan Pico, were especially important consultants and provided details about life on the Northern Channel Islands.[2] Written records from Spanish missions also provide data on baptisms, marriages, genealogy, and other aspects of Chumash society. These records are often fragmentary, but they offer a fairly detailed picture of aspects of Chumash lifeways. Anthropologists like Travis Hudson, John Johnson, and Jan Timbrook of the Santa Barbara Museum of Natural History; Thomas Blackburn of California State Polytechnic University at Pomona; Lowell Bean of California State University at Hayward; and others have analyzed ethnohistoric records and used them to explore everything from Chumash genealogy and sociopolitical systems to place-names, healing practices, ceremonies, and rituals.[3] A growing number of Chumash tribal members are also investigating their own oral histories and ethnohistoric records to explore and reinvigorate their cultural heritage, language, and identity. Archaeology and ethnohistoric accounts provide interrelated and complementary perspectives for illuminating the deep history of Chumash occupation of the Northern Channel Islands.

The most intensely studied interval of Northern Channel Island history is the Late Holocene, from about 4,000 years ago to the present. Numerous researchers have worked to decode how, why, where, and when the Chumash society described in ethnohistoric accounts came to be. Interpreting transitions in technologies, subsistence patterns, and social organization has required the use of finer-scale temporal designations (Late Period, Middle Period, etc.) to subdivide this time period, but we simplify matters by relying on specific calendar ages to discuss important events of the Late Holocene, with two exceptions—the Protohistoric and Historic periods. The Protohistoric Period refers to the interval of sporadic Chumash contact with Europeans, beginning with the maritime Cabrillo expedition in 1542–1543 CE, which lasted for 227 years until 1769 CE when Spanish colonization of Alta California began. For the Island Chumash, the Historic Period (aka Mission Period) spans about 50 years, from 1769 CE to the early 1820s, when the surviving Island Chumash were removed to mainland missions and pueblos. The Protohistoric and Historic periods are the focus of chapter 6, but we briefly discuss them here to contextualize key cultural and environmental developments of the Late Holocene.

This chapter builds on our earlier discussions of the Paleocoastal colonization of the Northern Channel Islands and the important cultural and environmental transitions of the Middle Holocene. Changes in human settlement and social organization, subsistence and diet, and technologies all accelerate in the Late Holocene. It is a time of pronounced growth in human populations, a shift to greater sedentism, more formal social hierarchies and inherited (hereditary) leadership, increasingly elaborate material culture, and greater human influence on land and seascapes. Part of what makes the Late Holocene so interesting is the acceleration of human cultural developments alongside changing environmental conditions, such as droughts and El Niño events. We explore each of these developments in turn, beginning with human settlement dynamics, village formation, and territoriality, followed by changing social organization, technology, exchange and subsistence systems, environmental fluctuations, and human health.

SEDENTISM, VILLAGES, AND SETTLEMENT DYNAMICS

A defining characteristic of island settlement patterns from Paleocoastal to Middle Holocene times is human mobility that relied on regular movement across the landscape to access resources, perhaps seasonally. With some notable exceptions discussed in chapters 3 and 4, earlier

people were probably relatively mobile, and large, permanent communities were limited. The past 4,000 years on the islands, particularly
the last 1,500 years, saw a pronounced increase in sedentism, meaning
sustained occupation of a specific area, the formation of more or less
permanent villages, and increased territoriality—sometimes resulting in
violent conflict.

Where and for how long people choose to settle is an important part
of human demography and decision making. Prior to about 1,500 years
ago, most human settlements shifted regularly to take advantage of
productive resource areas scattered across land and seascapes. By 3,000
to 2,500 years ago, however, large villages were established at some key
locations. The earliest part of the Late Holocene remains poorly studied, but a picture of growing populations and a society in transition has
emerged over the last decade or so.

At Cuyler Harbor on San Miguel Island, archaeological investigations
at a massive archaeological site known as CA-SMI-87 in the late 1990s to
the early 2000s provide a window into this transition.[4] This site, located in
prominent dunes above a beautiful sandy beach and freshwater springs,
covers an area of more than 10 acres (40,000 square meters). Although
lacking clear house features like classic Island Chumash villages, the site
contains large rock platforms that likely functioned as cooking areas, living
floors, or platforms for drying or processing foods. An important aspect of
this site is the sheer volume and density of tool-making debris (stone and
bone), dietary refuse (shellfish, fish, bird, and marine mammal remains),
and other materials. CA-SMI-87 has all the makings of a sedentary village
but lacks many of the key hallmarks we see later in time. The site also
contains earlier Middle Holocene deposits that suggest more specialized
activities like red abalone processing, further supporting a transition to a
more sedentary community around 2,500 years ago.

On Santa Cruz Island, this early interval of the Late Holocene also
is a time when human settlements increase in scope and magnitude.
California State University at Channel Islands archaeologist Jennifer
Perry has suggested that population growth, increasing competition, and
resource stress around 3,000 years ago resulted not only in greater sedentism on Santa Cruz but also expansion into less optimal habitats such
as less resource-rich stretches of the Santa Cruz Island interior and coast
and onto smaller islands like Anacapa.[5] Archaeological investigations on

East Anacapa seem to support this pattern. East Anacapa contains four archaeological sites, all occupied between about 3,500 and 2,500 years ago. Each site has produced evidence for a range of activities, similar to those seen at CA-SMI-87, including tool production from deer bones that suggests increased trade with mainland neighbors.[6]

Drawing on aspects of human behavioral ecology (the study of human behavior from an ecological and adaptive perspective), Douglas Kennett and University of Nevada at Reno archaeologist Chris Jazwa found similar Middle and Late Holocene settlement patterning. Many of the largest and most prominent island drainages, like those on the northwest coast of Santa Rosa Island, were occupied continuously from the Middle Holocene into the early Late Holocene, between about 3,000 and 1,500 years ago.[7] However, Islanders also established settlements near smaller, less prominent drainages to facilitate access to important subsistence resources such as the seal and sea lion rookery on western San Miguel Island.

Between about 1,500 and 200 years ago, the Channel Islands witness the full range of Chumash activities documented by early European explorers. Nowhere is this more apparent than in human settlement dynamics and village formation. Ethnohistoric sources and mission records document 21 named Island Chumash villages, found on all of the Northern Channel Islands except Anacapa[8] (figure 5.1). Several studies have correlated ethnohistoric locations with the presence of large archaeological village sites that contain evidence of historical occupation (glass-drilled or metal needle–drilled beads, Historic Period radiocarbon dates, metal tools or European artifacts, etc.). Specific archaeological sites or groups of sites have been linked to most of these named villages, providing a degree of confidence in our understanding of Historic Period Chumash settlement. These villages each contain house depressions or other domestic features and massive shell middens and other refuse deposits, attesting to large village populations; intensified fishing and other subsistence activities; surging bead, fishhook, microblade, and other technological production; and a suite of other activities. Nearly all these villages have been recorded along prominent and resource-rich island coastlines, but an additional, perhaps seasonal, village (*Nimatlala*) recently was identified by archaeologist Elizabeth Sutton on interior Santa Cruz Island.[9]

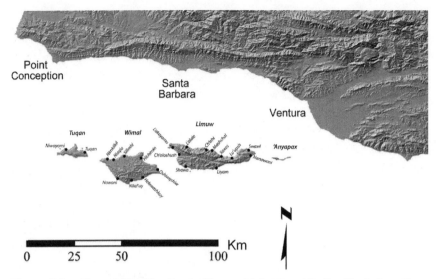

Figure 5.1. Map of the Northern Channel Islands with the likely locations of the 21 historical Chumash villages. Note that several village locations remain tentative, and continued archaeological investigations will be necessary to determine their most likely locations at historical contact. *Source:* **Todd J. Braje.**

An interesting component of these Historic Period villages is that most contain evidence for human occupation dating back to at least 1,500 years ago (and in some cases much longer) either at the same site or an adjacent site, suggesting that settlement dynamics were in place for several millennia. After roughly 1,000 years ago, following a model described by Kennett and Jazwa, the Chumash increasingly consolidated settlements at key coastal village sites. For several decades, University of California at Los Angeles archaeologist Jeanne Arnold and her colleagues investigated the nature of Late Holocene Chumash settlement and village formation on Santa Cruz Island, particularly over the last 1,500 years. Her work at important sites like CA-SCRI-192 (the village of *Shawa*) at Morse Point on southwest Santa Cruz and at CA-SCRI-233 (*Xaxas*) at Prisoners Harbor confirms this trend of settlement continuity at strategic locations across the past 1,500 years (figure 5.2).

While village formation, increasing sedentism, and territoriality define the period from about 1,500 to 200 years ago on the islands, people continued to use smaller seasonal or satellite camps for fishing, hunting marine mammals, and gathering shellfish and plant foods. In

Figure 5.2.   Photograph of the sea cliff exposure at the historical village of *Shawa* **on Santa Cruz Island. Note the dense shell midden eroding onto the beach below.** *Source:* **Torben C. Rick.**

particular, important quarry sites on Santa Cruz and other islands contain evidence for the mining of high-quality cherts. These raw materials were used to produce stone microdrills for perforating shell beads, as well as for other stone artifact production. While the focus of many archaeologists investigating Late Holocene sites on the Channel Islands has been village locations, several surveys demonstrate that smaller sites on the coast and in the interior continued to be a central part of settlement and land use strategies.

This pattern is well documented on Anacapa Island, where a few sites were occupied during the past 1,500 years, including at least two caves with Historic Period Chumash occupation. Similar to earlier Anacapa settlement, people probably occupied this island as a satellite location from adjacent Santa Cruz Island or the mainland. However, a few sites, especially on Middle Anacapa Island, contain large and dense archaeological deposits, suggesting more sustained occupation and a primary village. Collectively, the Late Holocene settlement system was dynamic with periods of rapid change, especially with the increase in villages' coalescence around high-ranked drainages, and increased territoriality beginning about 1,500 years ago and continuing into the last 200 years.

SOCIAL INEQUALITIES AND HIERARCHIES

Along with changing settlement dynamics came new developments in human social organization. The Chumash of the Santa Barbara Channel area are famous for their large villages, inherited chiefly leadership, and hierarchical social organization, patterns fairly unique for nonagricultural hunter-gatherers. The Chumash are often compared to the Calusa of Florida and many of the coastal hunter-gatherer tribes of the Pacific Northwest, who also had high population densities and distinct social hierarchies. Due to these unique developments, several researchers have focused on understanding the origins of Chumash chiefly leadership and social dynamics, often called emergent complexity. Although the precise structure of Chumash social hierarchy remains debated, Chumash villages were a key part of their social organization, with inherited leadership and some village chiefs exerting at least a degree (perhaps much more) of influence or control over other villages and both men and women serving as chiefs.

When, why, and how patterns of emergent complexity appeared among the Island Chumash has been hotly debated by archaeologists. Key among these questions is how archaeologists determine aspects of social organization in the archaeological record. Although archaeologists today generally do not excavate human remains or burials on the Channel Islands, past archaeologists excavated and analyzed human remains. Today, Native American burials, funerary objects, and human remains are protected by federal law, and archaeologists work closely with Native American tribal members, including the Chumash, on all aspects of archaeological research. With very rare exceptions, human remains are not disturbed, and their locations are protected. Still, past excavations of human remains, mostly prior to the 1970s, have helped archaeologists glean important information about human social organization. For instance, archaeologist and Chumash bead expert

Chester King, Lynn Gamble, University of California at Santa Barbara bioarchaeologist Phillip Walker, and others noted that some Chumash burials contain greater numbers of and more elaborate grave goods and wealth items than other burials. This includes the amount and type of shell beads, shell and bone ornaments, and other specialized items that signify wealth and status. Changing burial patterns and associated grave offerings reflect aspects of increased hierarchy and appear on the Northern Channel Islands after about 1,500 years ago, although antecedents are seen earlier in time as well. Assessments of burial goods and status are one important variable for tracing the rise of social inequality, but archaeologists also consider changes in human settlement, territoriality, exchange, subsistence, and other aspects of human society that reflect social organization.

Although Island Chumash social organization evolved considerably during the Late Holocene, similar to changing settlement systems and territoriality, the most pronounced changes in social organization occurred between about 1,500 and 200 years ago. By about 800 years ago, all aspects of Chumash society observed by European explorers and later described by Chumash community members like Fernando Librado Kitsepawit were in place. This ushered in the Late Period, essentially the "classic" Island Chumash culture. The preceding 700 years or so are often seen as a tumultuous time, referred to as the late Middle Period and Middle-to-Late Transition.

One model holds that the Chumash had to respond to a series of marine catastrophes and extended El Niño events that created warmer than average ocean temperatures and reduced marine productivity. These climatic events forced people to coalesce around productive watersheds and drove increasing hierarchy and exchange.[10] This model was challenged when a new marine climate record suggested much the opposite. Although variable, this interval was characterized by relatively cool ocean temperatures and highly productive marine environments. Attention then turned to the potential effects of droughts,[11] while other archaeologists viewed developments between about 1,500 and 800 years ago as a continuation of a long period of change and development, population growth, and social interaction.[12] Each model has strengths and weaknesses, but all agree on a few key variables. First, Chumash social organization changed rapidly around 1,500 to

700 years ago, and territoriality and exchange facilitated hierarchical social organization. Second, all agree that environmental change influenced social change, but each model differentially emphasizes specific environmental events.

Which model is correct? Archaeologists struggle to develop precise models to explain social and political change. We are often plagued by equifinality, where multiple conditions can result in the same outcome. Each new research finding, new climate record, and other data source improves our models and moves us closer to a more nuanced picture of the human past, but there will always be debate. Arguments over the primary driver of Island Chumash social organization will persist, and they mirror similar deliberations about other human societies such as the rise and subsequent dramatic reorganization of the ancient Maya. One thing we can say with certainty is that Chumash cultural changes after 1,500 years ago were rapid, and the ensuing centuries witnessed the development of the classic Island Chumash way of life, with hierarchical social organization (including inherited vs. earned status), sophisticated patterns of exchange and craft production, and distinct subsistence pursuits focused on a range of marine and terrestrial foods.

With the attention given to the past 1,500 years of Island Chumash archaeology, the previous 2,000 years are often lost in the shuffle. Between about 4,000 and 1,500 years ago, social organization remains poorly understood and is an area that needs greater attention from Channel Island archaeologists. This interval likely differed from the social organization of the Middle Holocene, as aspects of human social life may have changed with an increasingly sedentary lifestyle and the formation of villages at some key locations. Similarly, as subsistence activities diversified and there was a greater emphasis on fishing, the distribution of labor and other aspects of social and political dynamics likely changed. Still, other crucial variables, especially craft production and exchange had not dramatically changed from earlier times, particularly compared to the period after 1,500 years ago. The early portions of the Late Holocene likely set the stage for the dramatic changes of the last 1,500 years, and future research should help us better understand evolving Chumash social organization through time and space.

TECHNOLOGY AND EXCHANGE

The Late Holocene was also a time of rapid technological innovation. With changes in social organization and demography, new technologies appeared, many of which were refinements of existing tools. Other long-standing technologies (e.g., beads) began to be mass produced. Although technological changes were widespread, five developments were particularly revolutionary in spurring changes to Island Chumash society: (1) the *tomol* or plank canoe used to transport people and goods across the Santa Barbara Channel and for fishing and other activities; (2) single-piece fishhooks made of shell or bone spread rapidly to become one of the most ubiquitous and important technologies in the region; (3) the toggling harpoon, which may have helped capture swordfish and other large marine animals; (4) the bow and arrow, which became a central technology for hunting and interpersonal violence; and (5) *Olivella* shell money beads (and the stone microdrills used to produce them), which facilitated regional trade (nearly all of which were produced on the Northern Channel Islands) (figure 5.3).

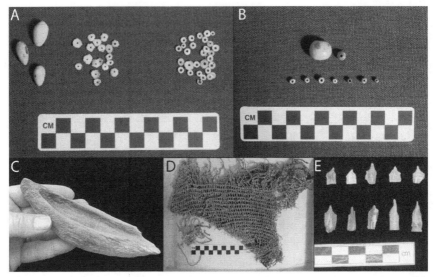

Figure 5.3. Photographs of Late Holocene technology from the Northern Channel Islands: (A) money bead production sequence: whole *Olivella* shells, rough-chipped beads, and finished callus cup money beads; **(B)** glass beads from CA-SRI-2 on Santa Rosa Island; **(C)** a model canoe from CA-SRI-6 on Santa Rosa Island; **(D)** a woven sea grass bag from CA-SRI-2; and **(E)** microdrills used for bead construction from San Miguel Island. *Source:* Torben C. Rick.

Watercraft were an important part of human life on the Northern Channel Islands since initial colonization. Most boats are made of perishable materials (wood, reeds, animal hide, etc.), however, so we know little about the specific types people may have used prior to ethnohistoric records. Ethnographic accounts suggest that the Chumash used at least three types of watercraft: tule reed boats or balsas, small dugout canoes, and *tomols* or plank canoes. Tule reed boats were excellent for nearshore fishing and transportation in shallow waters. Little is known about Chumash dugout canoes, and they may have been rare given the lack of suitable wood for their construction. The *tomol* was the most seaworthy of these boats and ideal for travel between the islands or to the mainland.[13] They also served well for kelp forest and deep-water fishing and other marine subsistence activities. Based on ethnographic accounts, *tomols* could be up to 9 meters long, carrying numerous people and a variety of trade goods.

Tomols were made from planks split from redwood logs, sewn together and waterproofed with asphaltum (bitumen) and pine pitch. *Tomols* and *tiats* (the name for similar sewn plank boats among the Gabrieleño-Tongva of the Southern Channel Islands) are among a handful of plank boats made by Indigenous groups around the world, including the Marshall Islands in the Pacific and in parts of coastal Chile. In southern California, where wood is scarce, *tomols* were an ingenious invention that relied on drift redwood logs transported southward by the California current from trees eroded out in central and northern California. Fragments of carefully shaped *tomol* planks, often painted with red ochre, are occasionally found in island archaeological sites.[14] The Chumash name for Santa Rosa Island is *Wima*, which roughly translates to "driftwood." *Tomols* were very seaworthy, with some accounts suggesting that people could travel from the islands to the mainland in four to six hours. This ingenious invention helped fuel complex interaction and exchange networks.

More than simply functional tools, *tomols* also held ritual significance for the Chumash. A guild called the Brotherhood of the Tomol included special members of Chumash society charged with building, using, and caring for these important boats. The Brotherhood were the keepers of sacred knowledge on how to build a *tomol,* and elite Chumash individuals with access to wealth and influence had to strike a deal with the Brotherhood if they wanted a *tomol* constructed. Once completed, the watercraft could be used to transport trade goods and items of status and wealth from the mainland to the islands, and leveraged into sizeable profits and increased social status for its owner (sidebar 5.1).

Bridging the Northern and Southern Channel Islands by René L. Vellanoweth, California State University, Los Angeles

The Northern and Southern Channel Islands are more alike than they are different and have similar archaeological records with roughly parallel environmental and human histories. Despite differences, the islands are home to similar types of shellfish, fish, marine mammals, and birds. All contain different amounts of freshwater and enough useful plants, sea grass, and kelp to subsist and produce and maintain fire. Glue in the form of asphaltum washes up on northern and southern island beaches and stone outcrops provide raw material for making tools. These and other resources made it possible for humans to survive on the Channel Islands for millennia, and all people—from the Chumash and Gabrieleño-Tongva, to the Spanish, Russian, and American—had to take advantage of opportunities and overcome obstacles to sustain themselves. The Chumash and Tongva of the area were particularly good at this and left behind a rich and diverse archaeological record.

Antiquarians and archaeologists have been uncovering evidence of past human activity on the Channel Islands for nearly 150 years. The material culture and technological traditions of the Island Chumash and Gabrieleño-Tongva were typically based on what could be obtained from the immediate environment, which produced similar types of artifacts and industries. Shell beads, for example, followed comparable stylistic trajectories for each island group and, over time, created the backbone for regional and long-distance exchange networks. In both places, beads were produced locally, traded widely, and functioned to maintain creative expression, group cohesion, and cultural affiliation.

Although distinct worldviews among northern and southern peoples existed, their ceremonies were supported by common ritual paraphernalia, such as stone pipes, iron concretions, and charmstones, which have been found across the Channel Islands. Intermarriage, barter, trade, and other political and economic events brought Indigenous communities together, helping maintain social bonds and a cohesive regional culture that can be seen in the archaeological record today. These similar traditions, rooted in the building blocks of the islands themselves, provide a

Figure 5.4. Historical photograph of Fernando Librado, a Chumash consultant who was born at Mission San Buenaventura in 1839, directing the construction of a *tomol* in 1912. Plank canoes were critical for facilitating trade and interaction between the northern and southern islands and the mainland. *Source:* open access image via islapedia.com.

unique opportunity to explore a variety of historical and ecological questions and issues (figure 5.4).

The appearance of *tomols* occurs alongside other technologies. Some archaeologists believe that compound harpoons were first used in the Santa Barbara Channel area around 2,500 years ago; however, these dates are not yet definitive. Compound harpoons had a foreshaft with a barb and point that separated from the handle after being embedded in a large fish or marine mammal. This foreshaft was attached to a line and a float (usually a sea lion or seal bladder); after spearing their prey, people could hold on from a boat and tire the animal before taking it to shore. Archaeologists have suggested that compound harpoons, along with *tomols*, were important technologies that allowed the capture of large pelagic fishes, like swordfish, which were of ritual significance to the Chumash.[15] East Los Angeles College archaeologist Julie Bernard reviewed the occurrence of swordfish, tuna, mako shark, and other "trophy fishes" in Channel Island archaeological sites. She found that their occurrence increased dramatically around 1,500 years ago, perhaps marking the widespread use of *tomols* and compound harpoons.[16]

Growing populations in the Late Holocene meant more food was needed to fuel expanding Chumash communities. One of the most pronounced changes, particularly after 1,500 years ago, is a dietary shift toward finfish as the primary source of protein, with reduced reliance on shellfish, marine mammals, and birds at most locations. People likely intensified the use of fishing technologies that had existed since the Early or Middle Holocene, including nets, bone gorges, and fish spears. By about 2,500 years ago, however, people began using single-piece fishhooks made primarily from mussel or abalone shell. These fishhooks were circular or j-shaped and, shortly after 2,500 years ago, appear across the Northern Channel Islands and mainland Santa Barbara Channel. Interestingly, similar hooks may have been used as early as 12,000 years ago on Isla Cedros in Baja California, Mexico, and by about 3,000 years ago on the Southern Channel Islands. It is not known if the Chumash adopted the technology from interactions with people to the south or if it was an independent invention.

Single-piece fishhooks are one of the most common artifacts, along with shell beads, found in Channel Island archaeological sites dated to the last 1,500 years. Their abundance is a testament to their importance for capturing fish in kelp forests, rocky shores, and other habitats. Archaeologist Roy Salls conducted experiments focused on the strength of a variety of natural fibers, noting that another important variable was the strength of the fishing line. Since the fibers used to make fishing line are perishable and rarely preserve in the archaeological record, archaeologists have inferred that yucca and other strong fibers were used, as well as woven sea grass or even human hair. Composite hooks used since the Middle Holocene, and fishing gorges used since at least 10,000 years ago, continued to be important technologies for the Chumash into the Historic Period.

The bow and arrow was a revolutionary technology used around the world that marks an important technological development beyond stone-tipped spears and darts. We noted in chapter 3 that Channel Island Barbed points (CIBs) fall into the size range of arrow points, raising the possibility this technology was used on the Channel Islands since the Early Holocene. While there appear to be a few waves of bow and arrow use in the Americas during the Holocene, the technology was not widespread in California until the Late Holocene, around 1,500 years ago. While the bow and arrow was used throughout Europe since the Late Pleistocene and in Arctic North America since the Middle Holocene, it is believed to be a relatively recent technological innovation throughout most of the Americas. When it did spread south from the Arctic, however, it was quickly adopted for the many advantages offered in both hunting and warfare. Bows and arrows, as opposed to spears and darts, are longer-range, more efficient hunting weapons. A hunter can more easily hide behind cover or attack from a kneeling position and can readily carry a quiver of a dozen or more arrows. The bow and arrow may also correspond with increasing interpersonal violence. Increased evidence of arrow injuries or deaths on the Northern Channel Islands roughly 1,500 years ago suggests that the bow and arrow correlates to a time when instability and violence were on the rise, and this deadly new technology may have exacerbated these patterns.[17]

While *tomols*, compound harpoons, single-piece fishhooks, and the bow and arrow were important innovations of the past 3,000 years, one of the most dramatic changes in Chumash technology was an explosion in bead making after 1,500 years ago. Beads were an important part of people's lives on the Channel Islands for at least 10,000 years. Some *Olivella* shell beads were produced and traded over great distances in the Early and Middle Holocene, but this was a prelude to the mass production of shell bead currency on the islands during the last 1,500 years. *Olivella* beads, made first from the thin "wall" portion of the shell into a disk bead, then around 800 years ago or earlier into a cup bead from the thicker "callus" portion of the shell, became a formalized currency for the Chumash—akin to modern money. Beads were made by the millions, the vast majority on the Northern Channel Islands. They could be used to purchase goods and services and were a symbol of wealth, power, and societal engagement.

Critical to efficiently producing money beads were the chert microdrills used to perforate them. Craft specialists produced both microdrills and beads, most of them living on Santa Cruz Island.[18] All of the Northern Channel Islands and parts of the mainland had people making shell beads, however, and many villages and Chumash people engaged in this massive island-mainland trade network.

Beads were traded far and wide, ending up in the Great Basin and the American Southwest, perhaps traveling even farther than Middle and Early Holocene beads. The key difference is that bead and exchange networks from 1,500 to 200 years ago signify an expanding and formalized economy, an emphasis on wealth and power, and an evolving Chumash society with specialists and organized labor. Beads were the medium of exchange for goods and services (as our federally issued coins and dollar bills are today), and the *tomol* provided the means to efficiently deliver those economic goods across the sea. Exotic goods, such as obsidian from inland volcanic sources, soapstone bowls from the southern islands or mainland sources, or chipped-stone tools fashioned from beautiful green or red mainland chert sources, are found for at least 11,700 years on the Channel Islands. During the past 3,000 years, and particularly after 1,000 years ago, however, the trade of large numbers of these high-status goods from the mainland coast, the Santa Ynez Mountains, Catalina Island, the Sierra Nevada Mountains, and beyond signify a growing mercantile economy with large-scale regional exchange and interaction spheres. These material and information exchange networks facilitated changes in social organization, settlement, and territoriality, all important steps in the creation of the classic Island Chumash way of life documented in ethnohistoric accounts.

SUBSISTENCE, ECOLOGY, AND HUMAN HEALTH

The Late Holocene also witnessed important changes in human subsistence and diet, interactions with and impacts on local ecosystems and organisms, and changes in human health. One of archaeology's greatest strengths is building a picture of human diet through time. Channel Island shell middens are full of the animal bones, shells, and plant remains that people consumed for food and other purposes (figure 5.5). Analyzing and identifying these materials allows us to reconstruct human diets and the ecosystems where people hunted, gathered, fished, and lived. New technologies like stable isotope analysis of carbon, oxygen, nitrogen, and other elements in animal remains allow scientists to reconstruct whole food webs. As noted in chapter 4, ancient DNA analyses can help us understand the evolutionary relationships of a variety of

Figure 5.5. Photographs of several Late Holocene sites on the Northern Channel Islands: (A) Rick at the dense 1,200-year-old deposit at CA-SMI-481, packed with shell, bone, and tool-making debris; (B) a whale vertebra eroding from the sea cliff at a site near Point Bennett on San Miguel's far western end; (C) a dense sea mammal bone bed at CA-SMI-232 on San Miguel Island; and (D) Rick at a Late Holocene dune site on San Miguel dominated by California mussel shells. *Source:* Todd J. Braje.

organisms, like island foxes and mice, through deep time. Collectively, this work allows us to explore the complexities of human interactions with the environment through time. Increasingly, archaeologists are working with biologists and resource managers to use this information to aid contemporary conservation efforts on the Channel Islands and beyond (see chapter 7).

The Chumash and their predecessors have long been categorized as hunter-gatherers, meaning that they obtained their food from wild plants and animals rather than agricultural crops. Most archaeologists now recognize that hunting and gathering is a broad category that overly simplifies human subsistence strategies. Many hunter-gatherers practiced some forms of cultivation, and all managed the resources around them to varying degrees. The Island Chumash, for instance, kept domesticated dogs, introduced plants and animals to the islands, used fire as a management tool, grew tobacco, and may have had other resource management strategies we are not yet aware of, themes we return to below.

Since Paleocoastal times, Island people had diverse diets and obtained most, or all, of their protein from marine foods. Most early sites are rich in shellfish, suggesting that people focused on gathering intertidal bivalves, snails, and other marine shellfish as an expedient way to obtain proteins that could complement terrestrial and marine plants, fishes, birds, and marine mammals. A few early sites show intensive use of fin-fish, birds, or marine mammals (see chapter 3), but these are generally rare until the past 4,000 years when we see an explosion in the types of foods that people eat. People continued to consume huge quantities of shellfish for the last 4,000 years, but a defining characteristic of the Late Holocene is an intensified focus on finfish. As populations grew during the Late Holocene, people required more food to meet their nutritional needs. We have already discussed this in terms of new technologies (single-piece fishhooks, plank canoes, etc.), but these changes are also evident in the amount and types of foods people ate and deposited at their villages and other sites.

Dietary reconstructions for the past 4,000 years show that finfish account for 70 to 90 percent of the overall contribution of dietary pro-teins, with shellfish, birds, and marine mammals generally being supple-mentary.[19] This is a dramatic departure from most Early and Middle Holocene shell middens, where shellfish contribute 50 to 90 percent of the protein represented. The switch makes sense when you consider that, with the necessary technologies, finfish can yield far larger and more stable amounts of food than shellfish. There were more fish in the sea to feed growing Island Chumash communities. With the necessary equipment such as fishhooks, nets, boats, and spears, fish are a logical solution to meeting the dietary demands of growing populations. There are trade-offs, however, as it is time consuming to construct and main-tain fishing tackle and equipment. Fishing is risky, and not every outing will be successful. It makes sense, then, that Early and Middle Holo-cene communities focused on easy-to-capture and abundant shellfish prey and turned to less-efficient and more difficult-to-capture finfish when growing populations strained traditional shellfish resources.

In addition to the abundance of fish bone in Late Holocene archaeo-logical sites, we also see this shift away from shellfish in measurements of shellfish sizes. Over the last 20 years, we have measured thousands of shells from four economically important shellfish species (black and red abalone, California mussel, and owl limpet) dated across the last 10,000 years on San Miguel Island.[20] Except for black abalone, all showed sharp declines in average size through time, with the most dramatic change in the Late Holocene, particularly after about 1,500 years ago. Each of these species, especially California mussel (probably the most important shellfish for Channel Islanders), continues to be consumed and does not disappear from shell midden deposits. However, the decline in size suggests increased human predation pressure. People were harvesting smaller animals through time, presumably because they were forced to gather younger individuals. Local shellfish communities were unable to keep pace with this intensified human predation. These size declines are a measure of increasing human impact on local organisms and eco-systems and demonstrate that people were a driver of past ecosystem change on the Channel Islands.

Several important studies in the 1990s improved our understanding of human diet and health and provide important context for understand-ing shifts in human diets, especially the increased reliance on finfish. Studies of human remains in museum collections, often done alongside federally mandated NAGPRA (Native American Graves Protection and Repatriation Act) inventories, were conducted in consultation with Chumash communities. Work by Phil Walker, Utah State University bioarchaeologist Patricia Lambert, and their colleagues offers important perspectives that rely on human skeletal analyses or stable isotopes from human bone to provide a picture of what people were eating. Lambert and Walker's analyses, for instance, showed human health declines and upticks in violence corresponding with changing social organization and greater competition for resources among the Island Chumash after about 3,000 years ago.[21] These studies identified higher incidences of anemia and infectious diseases associated with increasing dietary spe-cialization and the focus on finfish. Declines in health are accompanied by increased evidence of interpersonal violence such as wounds from being hit or clubbed, as well as arrows and other projectiles. Detailed analyses of human teeth across the last 4,000 years show a decrease in cavities or dental carries, suggesting a shift away from carbohydrate-rich plants in favor of more finfish and other proteins.

These changes in human diet, health, and violence are closely related to Late Holocene social change. They illustrate the tension between population growth and human ingenuity as new social organization, technology, and territoriality had profound consequences for human well-being. However, many of these studies show significant improvements in human health indicators and a decline in interpersonal violence after about 600 years ago, suggesting that environmental conditions and other variables improved. One theory is that severe droughts forced island peoples to aggregate around a smaller number of fresh water sources, leading to greater social stress, shortages in key resources, pollution of water sources and increased illness, and greater intergroup competition, territoriality, and interpersonal conflict. Like the modern world, the challenges we face in terms of climate change, disease, food security, and violent conflict are similar to those faced by past societies, including the Island Chumash.

While people increasingly focused on finfish, the fish they consumed remained consistent, and there is no evidence that the Island Chumash overharvested local kelp forests and sandy and rocky shore habitats. Fishes like California sheephead, rockfish, pile perch, sardines and anchovies, cabezon, lingcod, and others that are found on dinner plates and on restaurant menus today in California were harvested by the Island Chumash and their predecessors for 10,000 years. Few studies have investigated patterns in fish size through time, but a preliminary study of California sheephead and another on rockfish show some size declines through time, mostly during the Late Holocene.[22] The average size of these fishes was still considerably larger than those caught today, however, suggesting that Island Chumash fishing pressure was limited and more sustainable compared to modern commercial and recreational fisheries.

Today, most marine fisheries around the world are in a frightening state of decline, plagued by decades of overfishing, climate change, habitat alteration, pollution, and more. Daniel Pauly, a fisheries biologist in Canada, notes that one of the major issues facing commercial fisheries is what he terms "Fishing down the Food Web."[23] Pauly showed that, as commercial fishers overfished large, desirable fishes like salmon and cod, they work their way down the food web to lower and lower trophic levels and less desirable species. This has resulted in the serial depletion of fisheries around the world and cascading declines in marine ecosystems.

Building on this work, we were interested to see if fishing down the food web was evident on the Northern Channel Islands in the deep past. Review of a massive dataset of animal remains from San Miguel and the other Northern Channel Island archaeological sites dated to the past 10,000 years found the opposite pattern.[24] The Island Chumash appear to have fished up the food web, first emphasizing lower trophic level shellfish and working into finfishes very late in time. This culminates in the past 1,500 years as people capture small amounts of swordfish, tuna, and other large fish from plank canoes. This more sustainable pattern of "Fishing up the Food Web" may be a key factor in the long-term success of Island Chumash society.

Despite the emphasis on fish and shellfish, people also consumed large quantities of marine mammals and birds during the Late Holocene. The bones, feathers, and hides from these animals were also important for making tools, clothing, and, sometimes, shelter. Marine mammals were also prized for their oil and hides, and sea otter furs were an especially valued trade item for the Island Chumash. Seals, sea lions, and sea otters are found in many Northern Channel Island archaeological sites dating to the past 4,000 years. They tend to be most abundant on San Miguel Island, due in large part to the presence of an ancient rookery near Point Bennett and offshore islets where these animals could safely haul out and breed away from people.

Between 1,500 and 1,000 years ago, several Channel Island sites contain large quantities of Guadalupe fur seals and California sea lions, along with Northern fur seals and some Stellar sea lions and harbor seals. People may have been increasingly taking these animals from offshore rocks and sheltered coves aided by *tomols* and toggling harpoons. Sea otters were also hunted at this time, a pattern we talk about in chapter 4 and one that may have influenced shellfish and other resource abundance in kelp forests. After 1,000 to 800 years ago, nearly all Island Chumash archaeological sites contain at least small amounts of pinniped bones and a hyperabundance of finfishes, suggesting that local overexploitation of seals and sea lions likely pushed these animals to Guadalupe Island and other sheltered places with little or no human presence. Although some dolphin, porpoise, and whale remains (e.g., orca, grey, and sperm whale) are found in sites dated to the past 4,000 years, they are likely the product of limited hunting of small cetaceans and scavenging of large whale carcasses. The Chumash are not known to have hunted large whales, but whale ribs and other bones are common in many coastal sites on the islands.

Birds, especially marine birds, were another important food source for the Island Chumash. People hunted or scavenged a wide range of marine birds, especially cormorants, albatross, pigeon guillemot, common murre, auklets, and smaller numbers of gulls, pelicans, and other species. People consumed these birds and used their bones to produce awls, gorges, and other tools, and their feathers for capes and ornamentation.[25] Small amounts of eggshells have been recovered from some sites, demonstrating the collection and consumption of bird eggs. Birds were generally supplemental foods, but they were relatively abundant at some sites. CA-SMI-163, a Historic and Protohistoric village (possibly the village of *Tuqan*) near Cuyler Harbor on San Miguel Island had abundant bird remains (figure 5.6). Finfishes dominated the assemblage, but large amounts of breeding sea birds like murres and auklets were likely being captured at Prince Island, an important nesting area for sea birds today that is located just offshore from CA-SMI-163. The harvest of birds and marine mammals document that the Island Chumash were taking advantage of key resources available in their immediate territory. These could then be consumed locally or leveraged as a trade item with other villages.

Of course, people cannot live on protein alone, and consuming too much protein without other key nutrients can be lethal. Terrestrial plant foods were a valued source of calories and carbohydrates. Until relatively recently, archaeologists considered the Channel Islands to have been impoverished when it comes to plant resources. Recent studies have turned this idea on its head, however, showing that island plant foods were critical sources of nutrition and medicine. One of the most important findings has been the abundance and nutritional value of geophytes (corms, tubers, roots, etc.), especially *Brodiaea* or blue dick corms, on the islands.[26] Archaeologist and paleobotanist Kristina Gill has demonstrated that blue dick corms were one of the most common plant

Figure 5.6. Overview of the village of *Tuqan* near Cuyler Harbor on San Miguel Island. Inset image is a map showing the remnants of the semi-subterranean house pits that are still visible on the lower terrace. *Source: Torben C. Rick.*

types consumed by the Island Chumash.[27] Today, these carbohydrate- and calorie-rich corms produce a beautiful flower that transforms island grasslands into seas of purple in the spring. The corm can be harvested with a digging stick, then eaten raw or roasted and consumed as an excellent source of carbohydrates and other nutrients. Gill recently identified charred corms in one site going back at least 11,500 years, currently the earliest evidence of geophyte foods being consumed in North America. These geophytes were also a dietary staple for the Island Chumash for the past 4,000 years, a perfect complement to the protein- and fat-rich marine animal resources available on the islands (sidebar 5.2).

People and Plants on California's Channel Islands by Kristina M. Gill and Jon M. Erlandson, University of Oregon

For more than a century, most archaeologists and other scientists described the Channel Islands' unique vegetation communities as impoverished compared to the adjacent mainland. Even Spanish accounts from

the 18th century suggest that the Island Chumash had few locally available plant foods. How did the Island Chumash survive for more than
10,000 years on islands lacking abundant plant foods? Did they travel to
the mainland to collect staple plant foods such as acorns, or rely on trade
with their mainland neighbors?

For decades, the idea that the islands were relatively marginal for
humans compared to the mainland shaped archaeological interpretations.
However, the recent recovery of island plant communities after more
than a century of heavy grazing by introduced sheep, cattle, pigs, horses,
deer, and elk is turning this idea upside down. Extensive grasslands, which
the Chumash actively managed for millennia (including regular burning),
support a phenomenally abundant supply of carbohydrate and energy-
rich geophytes with edible bulbs and corms—the perfect complement
to rich marine resources (e.g., shellfish, fish, and sea mammals). Recent
analysis of charred plant remains from island archaeological sites also
shows that the Island Chumash and their ancestors relied on geophytes as
a dietary staple for at least 11,500 years.

Probably the most important of these were blue dicks (*Dipterostemon
capitatus*), sometimes called "Indian potatoes," which grow in a variety of
soils from near sea level to the highest peaks. On the islands, millions of
blue dicks bloom each spring, turning coastal and upland grasslands into
a gorgeous sea of purple. Nourished by winter rains and summer fog drip,
we witnessed blue dick superblooms on Santa Cruz Island throughout a
severe four-year drought. The large starchy corms, edible raw or cooked,
can be harvested nearly year-round, and they are remarkably resilient to
human harvesting. Today, the abundance of geophytes and other plant
foods on the islands has shifted our perspective from one of resource scarcity to one of food security. This perspective seems more consistent with a
very early human presence on the islands, the abundance of Paleocoastal
and later sites, and the richness and resilience of Island Chumash culture
over millennia.

We have much to learn about Island Chumash harvest of corms and
other plant remains, but it appears that they significantly influenced
terrestrial ecosystems and plant communities, much the way they did
nearshore marine ecosystems. This probably included some management of blue dicks (intentionally replanting of small cormlets) and
other plant resources, possibly introduction of oaks and other plants to
different islands or parts of islands, and the use of fire as an ecological

management tool. Ethnographic accounts from the mainland demonstrate that the Chumash regularly burned landscapes to promote higher biodiversity and to create a balance between wooded and grassland habitats. There are no direct accounts of fire being used by the Island Chumash, but sediment cores from Santa Rosa Island show a dramatic increase in charcoal about 3,500 years ago, suggesting the use of fire as a Native American management tool.[28] Future research on fire and plant resources will help shape our understanding of Island Chumash lifeways and, ultimately, Channel Island ecosystems of the past, present, and future.

Other archaeological research demonstrates that food was not just a part of meeting basic sustenance for the Island Chumash. Jeanne Arnold and her colleagues documented a dense layer in midden deposits at the Chumash village of *Xaxas* on Santa Cruz Island that contained unusual quantitates of swordfish, black abalone, and other important foods. Arnold and colleagues believe this is evidence of a feasting event that brought Island Chumash people together for an important occasion or ritual. Similar evidence for periodic feasting has also been presented by Lynn Gamble on western Santa Cruz Island at a site dated a few millennia earlier (see chapter 4). Differentiating feasting and ceremonial events from the refuse of everyday life can be difficult, but communal gatherings and feasting for periodic ritual, social, and political events were undoubtedly an important part of Island Chumash life.

CEREMONIALISM AND RITUAL AMONG THE ISLAND CHUMASH

Ritual, ceremony, spirituality, and symbolism were vital parts of the Chumash world. We know a great deal about Chumash spirituality from the accounts of Chumash descendants in the late 18th and early 19th centuries. For instance, the Brotherhood of the Tomol was a guild centered around plank canoe construction, maintenance, and usage, the sacred knowledge of which was passed down through generations. Similarly, *'antap* was a secret society of Chumash religious and political leaders who conducted rituals and dances at major ceremonies, maintained a cosmic balance in the universe, especially through a winter solstice ceremony, and possibly created rock art. Chumash spiritual leaders were also community healers and conducted ceremonies for births, deaths, and other important life events.

While such information is difficult to decipher in the archaeological record, mission records and other ethnohistoric documents have identified Chumash singers and dancers from the islands.[29] One famous ethnographic account popularized in children's books and elsewhere tells the story of the Rainbow Bridge. This is an origin story for the Chumash, where *Hutash* (Earth Mother) created the Chumash people on *Limuw* (Santa Cruz Island) and later made a rainbow bridge for them to cross to the mainland. Chumash individuals who looked down during their trek fell into the water and transformed into dolphin brothers and sisters. These are just a few examples of the complex and important rituals, ceremonies, and traditional oral histories of the Chumash documented in ethnohistoric accounts, but they illustrate the breadth of Chumash worldview and how ritual and ceremony might manifest in the archaeological record.

The Chumash and their ancestors all practiced ritual, symbolism, and ceremony. These practices and behaviors are central to what makes us human, but they often tend to be less visible in the archaeological record. Archaeology's focus on material remains—those objects left behind and preserved to the present—poses challenges for understanding less tangible aspects of human behavior, including culture, customs, language, and religion. These are some of the most important and interesting parts of human cultures, however, and are central to defining who people were and how they viewed and constructed the world around them. Like many aspects of Chumash social organization, population growth, and exchange systems, Island Chumash ritual and ceremony become more apparent during the most recent 2,000 years, including evidence for rock art and portable ritual items and structures (sidebar 5.3).

Island Chumash Rock Art by Jon M. Erlandson and Kristina M. Gill, University of Oregon

Island Chumash life was rich in artistic expression, spirituality, and ceremonialism. One aspect of ritual and sacred practices is found in rock art, paintings (pictographs), and carvings (petroglyphs) found primarily in island caves and rock shelters. Mainland Chumash rock art sites, like Painted Cave in the hills above Santa Barbara, are famous for their elaborate, multicolored pictograph panels that often contain numerous abstract symbols. One of these (Pinwheel Cave) in the San Emigdio Mountains was recently shown to be associated with the use of the psychotropic drug datura.[30] Although not as common on the mainland, rock art sites are present on the Channel Islands, including Cave of the Whales on San Nicolas, which includes some 32 carved fish or cetacean motifs.[31]

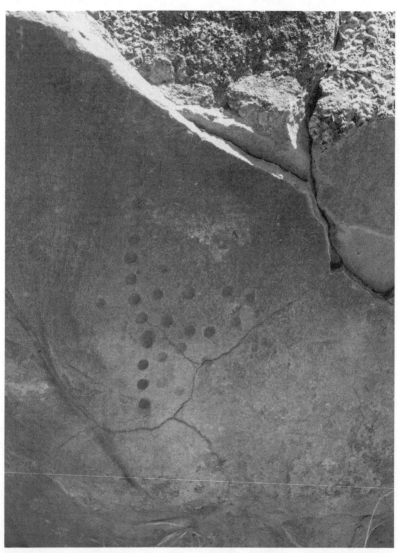

Figure 5.7. Photograph of the incised dots from CA-SRI-147, a large archaeological site on southern Santa Rosa Island. *Source:* **Kristina M. Gill.**

On the northern islands, for reasons not fully understood, rock art sites are relatively rare and generally less elaborate.

The former curator of paleontology and anthropology at the Santa Barbara Museum of Natural History, Phil Orr, was aware of the many elaborate mainland Chumash rock art sites and doubted that rock art existed on the Northern Channel Islands. He questioned the nature of the few reported sites, including two rock shelters on Santa Rosa Island containing incised grooves and dots. He believed these were utilitarian markings, created by grinding of bone, shell, or wooden tools. He also expressed doubts about the artistic nature of another site that contained only amorphous smudges of pigment on cave walls.

Two recently recorded island rock shelters suggest that such sites are the result of intentional rock art and ritual behavior among the Island Chumash. One, located near the south coast of Santa Rosa Island, contains incised grooves and dots similar to those Orr questioned, several of which are adjacent to an "aquatic" pictograph figure painted in red ochre (figure 5.7). The other rock shelter, located near the north coast of Santa Cruz, has smears of red and black pigment with little evident patterning, but also contains one clearly defined circular figure painted in black pigment.

These two sites demonstrate that the marks and pigment smears Orr questioned are associated with pictographs painted in Chumash styles. The dearth of island rock art may be due to limited research, poor preservation, or other processes, not the lack of such island rituals and ceremonialism. The function and meaning of island rock art is difficult for us to comprehend today, but the growing number of rock art sites suggests that the Island Chumash participated in many sacred rituals similar to those of their mainland neighbors and kin.

Archaeologist Jennifer Perry reviewed aspects of ritual and ceremony in the archaeological record of the Channel Islands, including both the northern and southern island groups, drawing on a rich collection of ethnographic and archaeological research.[32] This work provided descriptions of diverse archaeological evidence for Island Chumash ceremony and ritual, including large rock shrines, rock art, ceremonial or shamanic regalia, animal burials, portable art and ceremonial objects, and others. A ceremonial cache found on Santa Cruz Island, for instance, contained bone whistles, quartz crystals, stone pipes, an eagle claw, and red ochre. Stone shrines were an important element of Island Chumash ritual, and several examples have been recorded along a ridgeline on eastern Santa Cruz Island. These circular stone structures often contain a dark soil and abundant charcoal, which Perry interprets as evidence of burning wood or plants during rituals, such as the winter solstice ceremony (figure 5.8). Other archaeological correlates of ritual and *'antap* likely include bone whistles, bird feathers, stone crystals, ochre, and incised stones.[33]

Animal burials, especially dogs, island foxes, and raptors, were another important part of Channel Island ritual, with most examples coming from Gabrieleño-Tongva territory on the Southern Channel Islands. One example from San Nicolas Island documented by archaeologist René Vellanoweth contains a double dog burial with calcite crystals, ochre, and iron concretions known as *toshaawt* or sorcerers' stones, flanked by raptor and island fox remains.[34] A few dog and island fox burials have been discovered on the Northern Channel Islands, but none

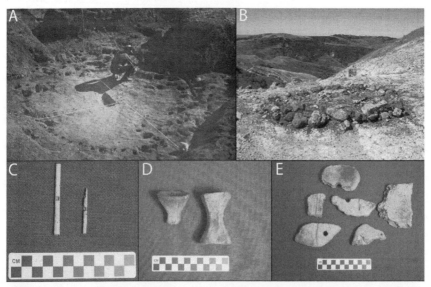

Figure 5.8. Defining characteristics of Late Holocene occupations on the Northern Channel Islands include the following: (A) the formation of large coastal villages with semi-subterranean houses like the one excavated by Phil Orr at CA-SRI-2 (*source:* open access image); (B) the appearance of distinctive ceremonial behavior such as the construction of rock shrines on island ridgelines (*source:* Sam Spaulding); (C) increases in ritual and exotic trade items such as bird bone whistles (*source:* Torben C. Rick); (D) swordfish "paint cups" (*source:* Torben C. Rick); and (E) comal fragments (*source:* Torben C. Rick).

contain the density of ritual items noted by Vellanoweth and at other Southern Channel Island sites on San Clemente and Santa Catalina islands.[35] An Island Chumash village at archaeological site CA-SRI-2, which may be the Chumash village of *Niaqla* or perhaps *Nimkilkil*, produced the remains of several dogs and at least one puppy, as well as a few island fox remains. Stable isotope analysis of these dogs showed that they were eating similar high-protein marine foods as people at the site, attesting to the close relationships between dogs and Chumash peoples on the Channel Islands.[36]

Aspects of gender also appear to have been tied to Chumash ritual, including the *'aqi*, a third gender among the Chumash that included biological males who dressed as females. The *'aqi* were associated with the undertaker guild, which did the spiritual work of a traditional undertaker for the dead.[37] Archaeologist Sandra Hollimon suggests that some Chumash burials on Santa Cruz Island may contain objects associated with the undertaker guild and *'aqi*, including spinal conditions that may have resulted from a life digging graves.[38]

Another aspect of Chumash ritual evident in the archaeological record may come from the remains of structures excavated in village sites. In chapter 4, we discussed the notion of persistent places, where people lived for long periods of time and evidence of ritual and ceremony are more likely to be found. At El Montón on western Santa Cruz Island, for instance, some 50 houses were accompanied by a separate cemetery with beads and other funerary offerings within individual burials, attesting to ceremonies and rituals associated with burial and death.[39] Archaeologist Lynn Gamble also identified what may be the remains of a dance floor and sweat lodge at the site. Collectively, these features and other materials uncovered at the site illustrate the linkages among feasting, ceremony, and ritual in the Middle to Late Holocene, activities that were likely pervasive throughout the Chumash world.

CONCLUSIONS

The Late Holocene was a time of dramatic change on the Northern Channel Islands and the broader Santa Barbara Channel region. It saw the appearance of the classic Island Chumash way of life first documented in European historical accounts. This includes increased sedentism, the development of formal villages that persisted for centuries to millennia, and increasingly hierarchical social organization. Technological developments like the *tomol*, single-piece fishhooks, and mass production of *Olivella* beads drove changes in subsistence, exchange, and regional economic systems. To complement abundant blue dicks and other plant foods, fish emerged as the most dominant animal resource, providing higher yields that fed growing populations. Human health declined and interpersonal conflict and violence increased after 3,000 years ago, but they appear to have improved after about 600 years ago. The Island Chumash had growing effects on local ecosystems and organisms, especially shellfish and marine mammals, but they also developed strategies for the long-term sustainability and resilience of local environments. The harvest of corms and use of fire as a management strategy provide important perspectives on aspects of Chumash environmental management and enhancement. The Chumash also had complex systems of ritual and ceremony, documented in both ethnohistoric accounts and the archaeological record. Starting in 1542 CE, European explorers and, later, Spanish missionaries traveled through the Santa Barbara Channel region, constructing several missions in the late 1700s. Introduced diseases, forced labor, and other aspects of colonial exploitation and oppression had severe consequences on the Chumash and Channel Island ecosystems, topics we focus on in the next chapter.

6

ISLANDS IN UPHEAVAL

For at least 13,000 years, the Chumash and their ancestors lived on the Northern Channel Islands and the adjacent mainland. Through the millennia, they developed a variety of new technologies for fishing, hunting, and seafaring. They expanded their populations across the islands, establishing large coastal villages led by chiefly lineages. They manufactured and traded shell money beads from the islands to the mainland, along trade networks throughout California, and into Baja California, Mexico; Nevada and Oregon; and points beyond. They introduced dogs and likely foxes to the islands and shaped island ecosystems through burning to create productive habitats for important plant resources. For more than 500 generations, the Chumash were intimately connected to the islands. They raised their children, passed down their stories and histories, performed rituals and ceremonies, and buried their dead. The islands were home.

One fateful fall day in 1542 CE dramatically changed life for the Island Chumash, when Juan Rodríguez Cabrillo, commanding three Spanish ships with a crew of 200 to 300 men—officers, seamen, soldiers, laborers, and slaves—made landfall on the Northern Channel Islands, likely San Miguel Island.[1] Roughly eight years earlier, Cabrillo was commissioned to build a fleet of ships to explore the coast north of New Spain, from Mexico to Upper California and beyond. The Spanish crown was interested in locating a northwest trade route to Asia and scouting lands for bounties of gold and riches similar to previous discoveries in Mexico and South America.

Cabrillo's expedition made landfall first in southern California near San Diego and on Santa Catalina Island. He also explored San Pedro and Santa Monica bays and the mainland Santa Barbara coast. After reaching Point Conception, strong winds forced Cabrillo to steer toward the Northern Channel Islands, where he found safe haven, probably in Cuyler Harbor. This marked the first known contact between European explorers and the Island Chumash, a brief event resulting largely by chance and circumstance, but one that had far-reaching consequences for native communities and island ecologies.

Poor weather forced Cabrillo and his crew to anchor for a week, passing the time attempting to decipher the island's geography and making much-needed repairs to some of the fleet's vessels.[2] While harbored at San Miguel, Cabrillo visited other islands, naming the principal island "La Posesión," probably either Santa Catalina or Santa Cruz island. Unfortunately, we may never know exactly which islands Cabrillo and his crew visited because Cabrillo's original log was lost, and later accounts used multiple names for the various islands they visited.

On October 25, 1542, as the weather cleared, the fleet resumed the expedition and headed north, exploring San Luis Obispo, Point Reyes, and the Russian River, but missing the entrance to San Francisco Bay.[3] On November 23, the adventurers returned to the Islas de San Lucas, "at one of those called Posesión," where they anchored and repaired the *San Miguel*, their leaking *fragata*. Most historians believe the anchorage was Cuyler Harbor on San Miguel Island, but all agree that Cabrillo's fleet wintered in a harbor at one of the Channel Islands, preparing for the return to Mexico.

Often overlooked in the broad brush of historical accounts of colonialism and exploration are the stories of Indigenous peoples. Indigenous communities are habitually assumed to have been willing or passive participants in the invasion and conquering of their worlds by European naval powers. Cabrillo, however, did not encounter awestruck or docile Indigenous communities on the journey up and down the California Coast. Similar to many places around the world during the Age of Exploration, Indigenous populations often resisted and repelled intrusion, even without the benefit of firearms and other European technologies. While Cabrillo's ships were anchored around the islands, the Chumash repeatedly fought with his crew. When Spaniards were searching for water on Christmas Day, a shore crew was attacked, and Cabrillo led a rescue mission. During this skirmish, Cabrillo reportedly broke his leg or arm. Gangrene soon set in, and the injury proved fatal. Cabrillo was buried on January 3, 1543, on an island his men called "Capitana." This may have been San Miguel, but no one knows for certain (figure 6.1).

After Cabrillo's death, chief pilot Bartolomé Ferrer (or Ferrelo) took charge of the expedition, leading the fleet north as far as Point Arena before turning south and arriving, battered and bruised, into their home port at Navidad on April 14, 1543. The Spanish crown viewed the

Figure 6.1. Arrival of a replica *San Salvador* to San Miguel Island's Cuyler Harbor in 2016, commemorating the first known contact between Europeans and the Chumash. Inset: View from San Miguel Island's Cabrillo monument that overlooks Cuyler Harbor and Prince Island. While still celebrated today, this moment was a devastating one for Chumash lifeways that resulted in tremendous upheaval for generations. *Source:* open access images via islapedia.com.

expedition as an utter failure: Cabrillo was dead, no hoard of gold or gems was recovered, and no northwest passage to Asia was found. The importance to California and its Indigenous people, however, cannot be overstated. For the first time in recorded history, a European had stood on California soil. Native California and the Northern Channel Islands would never be the same.

THE SPANISH INVASION

For the next 226 years, the Spanish crown was largely uninterested in exploration of the California coast and its islands, although sporadic contacts did occur. Beginning by at least 1572 CE, Spanish trading ships sailed once or twice a year between Manila in the Philippines, following trade winds across the North Pacific, then coasting south to Acapulco in Mexico. These dangerous four- to six-month "Manila Galleon" voyages were the economic lifeblood of the Spanish overseas empire. Eastbound galleons delivered Chinese silks, spices, and porcelains and Asian beeswax for Mexican silver. Westbound ships returned to Manila to buy more Chinese goods and provisions for a return trip to Acapulco. Departing from Manila, the galleons aimed for Alta California to avoid the notoriously stormy coasts of the Pacific Northwest. However, some strayed off course and were forced to negotiate a long and dangerous voyage down the coast. Some ran aground; some were taken by pirates; and some simply disappeared.

Recognizing the need for a port in southern California for galleons to escape pirate threats, re-provision, and make repairs from months spent at sea, Portuguese navigator Sebastian Rodríguez Cermeño was commissioned to explore the southern California coast during his navigation of the Spanish galleon *San Agustín* down to Acapulco. He wrecked while anchored in Drake's Bay at Point Reyes, but Cermeño and his crew assembled a launch and continued exploring the coast, including a brief visit to the Northern Channel Islands.[4]

Cermeño's exploration, like Cabrillo's, ended in failure, but Spanish administrators were undeterred. Botched missions reinforced the need for a safe port of call for cargo-laden galleons. In 1602 CE, Sebastian Vizcaíno, a pearl-fishing concessionaire, was commissioned to explore the southern California coast for potential ports. Vizcaíno set off with three ships from the southern tip of Baja California, making landfall on Santa Catalina Island and, in December, on the Northern Channel Islands.[5] Unlike Cabrillo's expedition, there are fairly detailed records from Vizcaíno's chronicler, Father Antonio de la Ascension, who described the islands and their occupants:

> When the fleet was in sight of the mainland, and near one of the islands, which was named "Santa Barbara" [Anacapa] the first of the channel, a canoe came flying out from the mainland with four men propelling it. Aboard was an Indian with his son and other Indians who accompanied him, who gave us to understand that he was the king or lord of that country.[6]
>
> [The Northern Channel Islands] are well settled with Indians who trade and communicate with each other and with those on the mainland. ... Between them and the mainland there is a very good and safe passage, so wide that in places it measures twelve leagues and at the least eight. This passage is named "La Canal de Santa Barbara" and extends from east to west. When those who came from China passed in view of these islands, they never thought them to be islands, because they were so close together, and therefore they kept away from them. We passed between them and the mainland as I have stated.[7]

Vizcaíno's expedition helped chronical physiographic features and the Indigenous communities of southern California, but it did little to expedite Spanish colonization of coastal California. Without the lure of gold, silver, and other precious commodities, the focus remained on regions to the south and the wealth generated from the Manilla galleon trade. For the Chumash and the other Indigenous communities of southern California, however, these contacts were likely influential and disruptive.

The potential harmful effect of these Protohistoric contacts in southern California and the Northern Channel Islands are still debated by archaeologists, historians, and other scholars. For some, the effects of early European visitations were transitory:

> Seemingly all the changes were minor: a few European words in languages, a few children of mixed blood, a few iron knives and pieces of cloth, perhaps a few ideas about Christian religion. Otherwise, there is little or nothing to indicate an important European influence among the Indians of California prior to the eighteenth century.[8]

There is some evidence, however, that contact with European maritime expeditions, including documented encounters with Cabrillo to Vizcaíno and potentially undocumented ones during the Manila Galleon trade, transmitted Old World epidemic diseases, which resulted in sharp population declines among the Chumash.[9] Native Americans, including the Chumash, were highly susceptible to deadly Old World diseases, including venereal, respiratory, and other infectious diseases common among the crews of European ships. Additionally, there were ample opportunities for disease transmission, especially during the wintering of Cabrillo's ships and large crews in 1542–1543 CE. With little or no immunological tolerance to these novel diseases, the effects could have been rapid, confusing, and devastating. It is impossible to calculate the number of deaths that might have resulted from these potential early epidemics. There is some archaeological evidence for a sharp decline in Island Chumash population in the century after the Cabrillo expedition, and one possible case of chronic syphilis has been identified for an Island Chumash woman buried within a decade or so of Cabrillo's visit. Other bioarchaeological evidence remains elusive as many of the diseases that killed millions of Native Americans after European contact leave no skeletal trace. The Protohistoric Period may have been a difficult time for the Chumash, marked by occasional foreign visitors with strange technologies, languages, and customs, followed by unexplained illness sweeping through communities.

By all accounts, however, Chumash communities on the islands and adjacent mainland clearly were thriving by the time the Spanish decided to establish a permanent foothold in southern California, beginning in 1769 CE. With Spanish colonization of Alta California, traditional Island Chumash lifeways that persisted and evolved for 13 millennia met their greatest challenges. Within just 50 years of Spanish conquest, Island Chumash culture ceased to function as it had for millennia, and island ecosystems faced threats unprecedented in their deep history.

THE MISSION PERIOD: THE SWORD AND THE CROSS

Spurred by fears of the territory being claimed by foreign powers, the Spanish began an aggressive colonization campaign of Alta California from San Diego to the San Francisco Bay in 1769 CE. The English had established colonies on the East Coast of the continent and modern-day Canada, and they sent exploration parties to the Pacific Coast. In pursuit of sea otter pelts and other valuable furs, Russian commercial traders were moving east from Siberia into Alaska, establishing bases in the Aleutian Islands, southeast Alaska, and, in 1805 CE, in northern California. Fearing they would lose their tentative claim to Alta California, the Spanish crown illegally took control of the region in 1769 CE with the title to the land, including the offshore Channel Islands, vested to the king of Spain under the Law of the Indies.

Spanish soldier and administrator Gaspar de Portolá was named governor of the Californias and tasked with directing an aggressive colonization campaign by land and sea to establish a series of missions, presidios (forts), and pueblos (towns) in Alta California. Friar Junípero Serra led Franciscan missionaries and enslaved Native Californians in constructing a series of missions and presidios. Two ships set sail from México, the *San Carlos* from La Paz on January 10, 1769, and the *San Antonio* from Cabo San Lucas about a month later. At about the same time, a land expedition departed from Loreto in Baja California Sur. This marked the beginning of the Spanish Mission Period in California, when a series of 21 religious missions were established between 1769 and 1833 from San Diego to the San Francisco Bay area. The first mission and presidio, the administrative and military arm of Spanish occupation, was established at San Diego in 1769, the second at Monterey in 1771. Four missions and a presidio were established in the Santa Barbara Channel area, including Mission San Buenaventura (Ventura today) and Presidio Santa Bárbara (a military post) in 1782, Mission Santa Bárbara in 1786, Mission La Purísima Concepcion (Lompoc today) in 1787, and Mission Santa Inés (Santa Ynez today) in 1804. Mission San Luis Obispo was founded in northern Chumash territory in 1772.

The missions were the epicenters of devastating changes that radiated like a series of tidal waves through Chumash society. Old World disease epidemics recorded by mission priests swept through Chumash communities, causing massive mortalities and disrupting long-established systems of local hunting and gathering, commerce and trade, and sociopolitical hierarchies. Between 1770 and 1796, Chumash communities between Gaviota and Cojo on the western Santa Barbara coast declined by 67 percent.[10] At the same time, cattle herds increased by between 400 and 500 percent,[11] making it almost impossible for the Chumash to maintain their broad hunting-gathering lifestyles that relied on expansive land area to hunt deer, elk, rabbit, and other terrestrial game and gather acorns, roots, fruits, and other native plants. The ecological fallout of Spanish livestock grazing on acorns, seeds, and other plant foods, foundational to Chumash subsistence, left Indigenous communities with little choice. Over several terrible decades, Chumash people abandoned their traditional communities and were increasingly incorporated into the Spanish agricultural and pastoral economy. Between 1786 and 1803, 85 percent of the documented Chumash conversions to Christianity and movement to the missions took place in the Santa Barbara Channel area.[12] During this tragic time, tens of thousands of Chumash people died from introduced epidemic diseases. Hundreds of survivors were forced into unsanitary, humiliating slavery-like conditions within the mission system, toiling away building adobe bricks, tending gardens and agricultural fields, herding cattle, and constructing the infrastructure of Spanish occupation.

Often celebrated as an idyllic time of progress and cultural cooperation, the reality of the Mission Period for most Chumash converts was death, disenfranchisement, and devastation. Venereal and other diseases and corporal punishment were common within the missions, and at least three major disease epidemics swept through the Santa Barbara Channel missions between 1797 and 1801: typhoid and pneumonia in 1797, an unknown illness in 1798, and pneumonia, diphtheria, and (possibly) pleurisy in 1801.[13] Tensions, uncertainty, and death led to Chumash revolts, which were quickly suppressed, with those involved severely punished. Diseases and high mortality rates pushed the Spanish to recruit more Chumash converts (neophytes) to facilitate their growing ranching and agricultural enterprises. In 1803, the viceroy of New Spain declared that all baptized Indians had to move to the missions rather than live in their home villages.

Initially, the Island Chumash were somewhat insulated from the worst of the Spanish mission system, although they suffered disease epidemics and high mortality rates. Spanish administrators and Junípero Serra decided not to build missions or outposts on the islands, and they agreed that the Islanders should not be relocated to mainland missions.

The Island Chumash were slow to arrive for conversion to mainland missions, with only nine recorded baptisms at San Buenaventura in its first four years. In 1804, church leaders considered building a mission on Santa Cruz Island; however, a measles outbreak in 1805 resulted in the deaths of more than 200 Islanders, and mission plans were put on hold. Slowly, with the breakdown of island-mainland trade networks, the ravages of disease epidemics, and the disruption of traditional lifeways, Spaniards forcibly relocated or Islanders reluctantly abandoned their homes for mainland missions and towns. Hundreds of Island Chumash eventually were baptized at mainland missions, mostly between about 1813 and 1817, with the last recorded baptism of an Islander in 1822. When the last Islander left for the mainland is unknown, some believe it was 1822, but there are reports of an unsuccessful Chumash resettlement of Santa Cruz Island after the Chumash revolt against the Santa Barbara Mission in 1824. By the late 1820s, Anacapa, Santa Cruz, Santa Rosa, and San Miguel islands had been vacated by the Chumash, who had called the islands home for at least 13,000 years.

Relatively little is known about the fate of most Chumash Islanders after missionization. The devastation of disease epidemics and the chaos of the Mission Period resulted in few historical documents or information sources, other than mission registers, census records, and early ethnographic accounts.[14] We do know that most of the Island Chumash who entered the missions were integrated into Missions San Buenaventura, Santa Bárbara, La Purísima, and Santa Inés. Once in the mission system, Islanders came under the authority of missionaries and *alcaldes* (elected leaders) selected from neophyte (Mission Indian) communities. Census registers suggest, however, that select individuals were recognized as *capitanes* (chiefs), and some traditional sociopolitical units and leadership structures were maintained following hierarchical and family structures from pre-mission island communities.

Between 1833 and 1835 CE, the Mexican government confiscated mission properties and exiled the Franciscan friars. The missions were secularized, and their extensive landholdings, supposedly held in "sacred trust" for the benefit of the Chumash, were sold or given away to private citizens. The surviving Islanders formed communities near the defunct missions and pueblos, fled to the interior, or attempted their own farming operations. For several decades, Channel Islanders lived apart from other Chumash communities, maintaining distinct sociopolitical units. Chiefs were chosen to represent important early island towns, even though these had been abandoned since the early Mission Period. Gradually, however, children of Islanders intermarried with mainland Chumash families, with non-Indians, or with native people from other parts of California.[15] The descendants of the Island Chumash persist today with several Chumash community members tracing their family genealogies to various Channel Island villages—a testament to the resilience of the Chumash people.

MARINE MAMMAL HUNTERS

By the time the Spanish began colonizing Alta California in 1769, Russian fur hunters had been operating in the Aleutian Islands in the far North Pacific for 25 years. In 1741, famous Danish explorer and navy officer Vitus Bering, while in Russian service, became stranded on the uninhabited Commander Islands, east of Kamchatka in the Russian Far East. Starving and desperate, crew members clubbed four sea otters. As history (or legend) would have it, one crew member, Fleet Master Khitrov, sold a prime collection of pelts at exorbitant prices to Chinese merchants after a harrowing journey in a makeshift boat back to Kamchatka.[16] Shortly after the return of Bering's surviving crew, Russian sealers and hunters began the wholesale slaughter of otters and other marine mammals in the Aleutians and Pacific Northwest.

Word of Russian hunting operations reached Spanish administrators, who responded by sanctioning a voyage to the northern frontier in 1774. Four years later, Captain James Cook sailed to the North Pacific, where his crew traded trinkets with Indigenous hunters for otter pelts. They discovered, as Russian hunters had earlier, that Chinese merchants would pay exorbitant prices for the luxurious fur. After a detailed report of Cook's voyage was published and widely circulated in 1784, fortune seekers from a variety of countries flocked to the North Pacific, creating a frenzy akin to the California Gold Rush nearly 75 years later.[17] For millennia, Chumash hunters had hunted seals and sea otters for their furs, meat, and bones without significantly threatening their long-term survival. The historical fur trade and commercial whaling and sealing operations that soon followed, however, would bring several marine mammal species to the brink of extinction, extirpate some species from local waters, and result in fundamental changes to California's kelp forest ecosystems.

The relentless slaughter of sea otters was driven largely by the market for their pelts in China.[18] Wealthy Chinese consumers cherished otter furs for their warmth and beauty, and otter fur became a status symbol in Chinese society. For more than a century, otter pelts dominated North Pacific commerce and trade. By 1790, a single pelt could fetch between US$80 and US$120 in China, in today's currency.[19] As the animals were hunted toward extinction, otters became increasingly rare and difficult to capture, prices rose, and pelts became ever more desirable. Even North American beaver pelts, the heart of the continental fur trade, could not compete with the elegance, opulence, and status of otter.

Market demand spurred exploration for fertile hunting grounds and rapid exploitation after promising locations were identified. Dense herds of otters could be found in the kelp beds, surf, and beaches in the far northwest Pacific but were scarce along the Oregon and Washington coasts. Once northern herds were hunted down, rich populations were discovered off the coast of California, and ship logs recorded abundant otters in kelp beds along the Santa Barbara Channel, especially around Santa Barbara and San Miguel islands.[20] English and American companies and individual hunters descended on southern California, many accompanied by Native Alaskan hunters and their highly maneuverable sea kayaks called *baidarkas*. These experienced hunters were experts at their trade, killing dozens of animals in just a few days, taking adults, juveniles, and pups indiscriminately. Largely abandoned by the Chumash, the Northern Channel Islands became an epicenter of the sea otter trade. Commercial hunting outfits regularly visited the area, and Native Alaskan hunters sometimes were left on the islands for months to harvest otters by the thousands.

The Channel Islands also became temporary homes for a colorful cast of characters, straight out of a Wild West movie. One of these was a Yankee frontiersman named George Nidever, born in Tennessee, who arrived in California with a party of "mountain men" via the first ever east-west crossing of the Sierra Nevada Mountains by white Americans (figure 6.2). Nidever settled in Santa Barbara and tried his hand at otter hunting, stock raising, and sheep ranching. He organized numerous successful otter hunts to the Northern Channel Islands, and he bought a ranching interest in San Miguel Island, where he lived in an adobe above Cuyler Harbor. Nidever's island adventures are legendary; many of these he recorded in his memoirs *The Life and Adventures of George Nidever*. In 1836, for example, during an otter-hunting expedition to Santa Rosa Island, Nidever and two companions engaged in a multiple-day shoot-out with a group of Native Alaskan hunters. In September 1853, Nidever sailed to San Nicolas Island on an otter-hunting expedition, where he and his crew located Juana Maria (the Lone Woman of San Nicolas Island of *Island of the Blue Dolphins* fame) and brought her to Santa Barbara. Just a few months later, Nidever rescued hundreds of stranded passengers from the wreck of the sidewheel steamer *Winfield Scott*, which ran aground on Anacapa Island in December 1853.

By the 1820s, frenzied hunting caused the otter industry to decline, and only a small group of persistent hunters were able to support

Figure 6.2. Remnants of George Nidever's adobe home on San Miguel Island. Inset: Mountain man, trapper, and rancher George Nidever. *Source:* **open access images via islapedia.com.**

themselves by 1870.[21] American whaleman and naturalist C. M. Scam-
mon wrote in an *Overland Monthly* article that only 2,600 sea otters
were captured along the entire coast of California in 1869. Scarcity
pushed market prices ever higher, and, by 1890, a single high-quality
pelt sold for upward of US$475 (~US$1,400 in today's currency) on the
London market. Skyrocketing prices allowed a small number of hunters
to continue the search for the remaining California sea otters until they
were hunted to near extinction and were locally extirpated from many of
their natural habitats throughout California, including all of the Channel
Islands.

As sea otter numbers waned around the Channel Islands, hunters
increasingly turned their attention to locally rich seal and sea lion communities for their pelts and fat. Prior to historical overhunting, tens of
thousands of seals and sea lions congregated on the beaches and rocky
shores of the Northern Channel Islands. Between about 1790 and 1835,
fur seals, in particular, were slaughtered by the thousands. Boat crews
of up to 20 men would land on beaches, especially on San Miguel Island
where the animals hauled out in large herds, killing seals with one or
two blows to the head with a club, a practice dubbed "knockdowns."
The fur was the most valuable product; however, the hearts, livers, and
meat of young animals were eaten, and the blubber from an adult could
be rendered into one and a half gallons of oil.

Other species also were targeted. Elephant seals were first hunted
in the 1880s, likely by whalers during the summer months when gray
whales left the Santa Barbara Channel. A single bull could quickly be
dispatched with clubs, lances, or musket balls and yield more than 200
gallons of valuable oil. California and Steller sea lions offered several
commercial products, fur pelts for luxury products, bull trimmings
(penis and testes) for the Asian medicinal market, blubber, whiskers to
clean opium pipes, and meat for dog food.

The historical hunting of otters and other marine mammals drove
these species to the brink of extinction. In southern California, commercial hunting resulted in the local extirpation of sea otters, Guadalupe fur
seals, and elephant seals.[22] Estimates suggest that between 500,000 and
900,000 sea otters were harvested from 1742 when commercial harvest
began and 1910 when a final, unsuccessful hunt was staged.[23] Fur seals
and sea lions endured a similar history as they were slaughtered by the

tens of thousands on the Channel Islands and broader North Pacific. Fortunately, all these species survived to repopulate the Channel Islands, but each suffered significant population size reductions (bottlenecks) and, in some cases, decreased genetic variability. DNA studies demonstrate that all sea otter populations suffered at least one bottleneck, and low levels of genetic diversity have been found in otters, elephant seals, and Guadalupe fur seals—all the result of historical overhunting.[24]

SHELLFISH COLLECTORS

The historical blitzkrieg of marine mammals in California and Northern Channel Island waters dramatically affected kelp forest and other marine ecosystems. In particular, the extirpation of sea otters from California Island waters—along with the disruption of traditional Native American economies—caused major changes in shellfish populations. The Chumash harvested mussels, abalone, and other shellfish species for more than 12,000 years, but the Spanish mission system, agrarian economy, and introduced diseases severely curbed this practice. Otters are veracious predators of shellfish, including sea urchins, crabs, abalone, and mussels. Because they lack the thick, insulating blubber of other marine mammals, they consume roughly 25 percent of their body weight daily in shellfish meat. An unintended consequence of the missions and fur trade was a veritable explosion in abalone and other shellfish populations released from normal predation pressures. For decades, abalone flourished and became incredibly abundant, especially black and red abalones.

Throughout the early 19th century, commercial maritime economies focused primarily on trade, shipping, and hunting for fur- and oil-bearing marine mammals. This was amplified mid-century when gold was discovered in the Sierra Nevada foothills, and fortune seekers from around the globe flooded the Bay Area and struck out into the mountains with hopes of discovering the mother lode. Chinese gold rushers were the single largest ethnic group to arrive in California during the Gold Rush, and most headed to the interior mountains and river valleys in search of gold.[25] The easy gold was quickly mined out, however, and competition for the remainder became fierce. Chinese immigrants became targets of racist attacks and political pandering—that the wealth of America was being stolen by Asian interlopers.

Many Chinese immigrants were pushed to the economic and geographic margins of the state, filling vacated positions as cooks, laundrymen, agricultural workers, laborers, and fishermen. A small group of pioneering Chinese fishermen discovered a California coastline overflowing with underexploited marine resources, many considered delicacies in mainland China, but largely ignored in California. Along with finfish, shrimp, seaweed, and other marine resources, Chinese fishermen began harvesting the black abalones that were now superabundant in rocky intertidal habitats of the southern California coast (figure 6.3). Using traditional skills and equipment, Chinese immigrants quickly dominated the abalone industry. They collected, processed, and dried abalones for export to other immigrants living in the United States or for overseas markets, such as China and Japan, where abalone fisheries were already depleted.

Figure 6.3. Archaeological evidence of Chinese abalone fishing on the Northern Channel Islands: (A) a dense pile of black abalone shells from a camp on western Santa Rosa Island; (B) a heavily eroded black abalone pile on southern San Miguel Island; (C) a historical circular rock hearth feature from western San Miguel Island; and (D) a reconstructed Chinese brownstone ware vessel and two glass spice bottles. *Source:* Todd J. Braje.

The first Chinese abalone fishing camps sprang to life in the San Francisco, Monterey, San Diego, and Baja California areas in the mid-1850s. Based on scattered historical newspaper accounts and archaeological excavations, we know Chinese fishermen established camps on Santa Cruz, Santa Rosa, and San Miguel islands by 1856, where they were dropped off for approximately three-month intervals. They often contracted with Euro-American–owned steamship companies to transport their products to domestic Chinatowns and, internationally, to China. At the peak of California's Chinese abalone industry in the 1880s, fishermen working the Northern Channel Islands processed roughly 40 tons of dried black abalone meat and shells annually, making it a multimillion-dollar trade.

For three decades, Chinese fishermen controlled the abalone trade until declining gold yields and depressed wages caused Euro-Americans to look to other industries. By the late 1800s, discrimination, exorbitant taxes, and exclusionary legislation combined to curb Chinese dominance. Hundreds of Chinese abalone fishermen worked the Monterey coast in the 1850s, but by the 1890s newspaper accounts describe them selling their boats and ending their harvests. The last of the Chinese abalone fishermen working the Northern Channel Islands hung on until the early 1900s. As they left the industry, the void gradually was filled by Japanese and Euro-American fishermen who expanded the fishery to include a variety of subtidal abalone species in Channel Island and other California waters, including red, pink, green, and white abalone. Abalone harvests continued on the Northern Channel Islands through much of the 20th century, primarily by Euro-American commercial outfits operating out of the Santa Barbara area, until the 1990s when overfishing and withering disease caused the collapse of abalone populations and the closure of a once thriving industry.

Archaeologically, the legacy of the Chinese abalone fishery can still be seen in scores of sites located along island coastlines that contain piles or scatters of large black abalone shells and occasional wood planks used to build drying racks, the remnants of rock-lined hearths used to boil abalones, or Chinese pottery fragments. Long ignored by most archaeologists, these historical sites are now regarded as one of the treasures of Channel Island archaeology, revealing details of a nearly forgotten history and a window into the nature of Channel Island nearshore ecosystems during the mid-to-late 19th century.

THE RANCHING ERA

No comparable interval in the deep history of the Northern Channel Islands caused more ecological change to island landscapes than the roughly two centuries of the ranching period, from the mid-1800s until the late 20th century (figure 6.4). Ranchers were first active on the islands during the Mexican-American period after the Chumash left the islands, but large-scale ranching operations were not established until after 1850. During the Gold Rush, thousands of entrepreneurs flooded the Golden State. Some struck it rich as miners, but many turned to other potential sources of wealth, including what became known as California's "other gold"—agricultural products. Commercial operations on the islands were small compared to massive mainland ranches, but their products quickly gained a reputation for premium quality.

Initially, sheep ranching was the dominant agricultural activity on the Northern Channel Islands. Sheep were first brought to California with

Figure 6.4. Historical photographs from the Channel Islands: (A) Otter Point on San Miguel Island in 1919 showing de-vegetation and dune activation resulting from sheep overgrazing (note the absence of marine mammals on the point and beaches) (*source:* open access image via islapedia .com); (B) historical structures that remain near Bechers Bay on Santa Rosa Island (*source:* open access image via islapedia.com); (C) the remnant olive grove on eastern Santa Rosa Island (*source:* Todd J. Braje); and (D) cattle grazing on Santa Cruz among a sea of introduced grasses (*source:* open access image via islapedia.com).

the Spanish missions, but cattle accounted for the vast majority of stock during the Mission Period. When California joined the United States in 1850, sheep ranching took precedent as the need for meat and wool sky-rocketed. Wool was critical for clothing and other textile products—with demand spiking during the Civil War years—and mutton and lamb pro-vided a ready meat supply. Fats were used for a variety of industrial uses, and stock was sold to provision other ranches. Overgrazing and drought caused booms and busts for sheep ranchers—including a severe drought in 1863–1864 CE that wreaked havoc on San Miguel Island (see below), but domestic and global demand spurred the industry until California ranked second in wool production (behind Texas) in the 1870s.

Santa Cruz Island produced a variety of premium agricultural prod-ucts, including wool; meat from sheep, cattle, and pigs; wine and grapes; and fruits, nuts, and grains. San Francisco businessman William Barron acquired the island in 1857 and established the first large-scale ranching operation, importing cattle, horses, and sheep. The operation grew to include 24,000 sheep before Barron sold the island to 10 San Francisco investors in 1868. Justinian Caire, a French immigrant and business-man, acquired all the Santa Cruz Island Company shares from his col-leagues by 1887. Over the next four decades, Caire and his family built a self-contained ranching community with a main ranch complex in the Central Valley that included housing, a chapel, a blacksmith shop, and a winery. Auxiliary ranch structures were also built at key locations across the island, along with wagon roads connecting them. To control soil ero-sion caused by grazing, farming, and road grading activities, numerous beautiful stone walls and check dams were constructed, many of which can still be seen today.

A diverse suite of exotic plants and animals was introduced, including fennel and pigs that soon went wild. The Caires created gardens and planted exotic trees, including eucalyptus, Monterey pines, cypresses, English walnut, peach, apricot, orange and lemon trees, oleanders, pepper and olive trees, acacias, and Italian stone pines. The most wide-spread introduced plants were exotic grasses, which took hold across the island to feed free-ranging livestock. In many ways, the landscape of Santa Cruz Island, along with the other islands, was transformed during the ranching period, an ecological and cultural legacy that looms large today.

Santa Rosa Island also supported a massive sheep ranch until the turn of the 20th century, then operated by the Vail & Vickers Company for nearly another century as one of the largest cattle ranches in the state. The ranching legacy on Santa Rosa began when the governor of Mexico granted the island to Jose and Carlos Carrillo, two prominent residents of the city of Santa Barbara. The Carrillo brothers showed little interest in the island and sold it to Carlos's two daughters and their husbands, Alpheus Thompson and John C. Johns. Thompson and Johns shipped the first livestock to the island in 1844 with 270 head of cattle, 51 ewes, two rams, and nine horses.

By 1859, litigation and episodic drought, a challenge that also wreaked havoc on mainland ranches, resulted in the removal of most of the cattle and sheep from Santa Rosa. That same year T. Wallace More, along with brothers Alexander and Henry, began purchasing Johns's shares until they owned the whole island by 1870. The More brothers developed a massive ranching operation on the island with between 40,000 and 80,000 head of sheep. Miles of fencing were erected, and ranching structures were built across the island. The center of operations was established at Bechers Bay, where the protected harbor allowed for maritime shipping and level land for productive ranching and agricultural activities. By 1873, a wharf was constructed at Bechers Bay to facilitate shipping, and 40,000 sheep were sheared that year. While the operation flourished, the Mores still had to overcome the significant challenges that came with sheep ranching in arid southern California. From 1876 to 1878, severe drought forced the Mores to slaughter tens of thousands of sheep, but they remained profitable by erecting two large boilers to render the carcasses for fat production. The slaughter left only 15,000 to 20,000 sheep on the island.

By 1881, Alexander More acquired full interest in the island and steadily increased the number of sheep, with the stock size swelling to as much as 100,000 by the late 1800s.[26] The shearing operation grew to industrial levels, provisioned by some 40 seasonal shearers, with experienced laborers able to produce up to 100 fleeces a day. Alexander's death resulted in litigation among his heirs and the eventual sale of the island to the Vail & Vickers Company in 1901, founded by two successful cattle ranchers from Arizona.

After lifelong business partners Walter Vail and J. V. Vickers pur-chased Santa Rosa Island, they began removing sheep and introducing young cattle that would graze on island grasses for one or two years, before being sold to mainland buyers. The Vail & Vickers operation took measures to contain the impacts of grazing cattle as they fortified old sheep pasture divisions, enhanced fencing, and avoided overgrazing by regularly moving cattle from pasture to pasture based on the availability of feed and water. Depending on the season and conditions, between 3,000 and 7,000 cattle were stocked on the island and transported to and from Bechers Bay pier aboard a boat equipped with a loading chute.

Around 1910, the Vails began importing deer and elk to the island for sport hunting. Elk were shipped in from as far afield as the San Joaquin Valley, Yellowstone National Park, and the Rocky Mountains; deer came primarily from the Kaibab National Forest. Until the 1970s, most of the hunting was done by island cowboys and friends and family of Vail and Vickers; however, a highly profitable commercial operation began in 1977 and continued until 2011. For nearly 100 years, the Company successfully operated on the island, and their legacy persists today. The National Park Service (NPS) has created a Santa Rosa Island Historic Ranching District in the Bechers Bay area to restore, preserve, and pro-tect the main ranch house, barns, schoolhouse, and other buildings from the Vail & Vickers era and tell the stories of island ranching in Channel Islands National Park (sidebar 6.1).

The Archaeology of Channel Islands Ranching by Jennifer E. Perry, California State University, Channel Islands, and Courtney H. Buchanan, Norco College

From the mid-19th through late 20th centuries, California's Chan-nel Islands were ranched and farmed by people of different national and cultural origins. They brought a variety of animals and plants with them to capitalize on the Mediterranean environments, bounded island landscapes, and positioning along maritime transportation routes. Their activities and values are inscribed into the islands' landscapes: picturesque ranch house oases framed by introduced fruit and cypress trees, sur-rounded by widespread erosion and habitat degradation caused by pigs, goats, sheep, and other nonnative animals. It is through historical archae-ology and ecology that we can better understand how ranching shaped the island environments we encounter today.

Beneath generalized portraits, both positive and negative, are variations in ranching practices across the islands and through time. Long-
term ranching operations existed on all the larger Channel Islands, but
they were more challenging and short-lived on smaller islands where
freshwater and other resources were limited. On Santa Rosa Island, the
Vail family managed a cattle ranch for nearly 100 years by using pasture

**Figure 6.5. Documenting the history of historical activities on
the Northern Channel Islands requires careful consideration of a
wide variety of archaeological evidence, including the following:
(A) historical ranching structures; (B) the graffiti left on historical
walls and objects; and (C) telephone poles, wiring, and other related
infrastructure.** *Source:* **Jennifer E. Perry.**

rotation and other sustainable ranching techniques that stand in contrast
to the devastation wreaked by sheep operations of former island owners.

On Santa Cruz Island, the Caire and the Stanton ranches were based in
the island's well-watered central valley; their operations overlay a concen-
tration of Chumash sites that span thousands of years. Satellite ranches
were dispersed across different microclimates, each supporting specialized activities: wine making at the Main Ranch, bread baking at Scorpion,
olive orchards at Smugglers. Connecting them were trails and roads,
boat and plane deliveries, as well as a still-visible telephone system that
functioned for a century. Evident in the ranch houses, barn foundations,
telephone poles, dams, trails, and other infrastructure is a knowledge and
prioritization of island resources that overlaps with Chumash lifeways.
Although technologies differed, one commonality across time is a focus on
freshwater. Remnants of water tanks, piping, troughs, and dams are often
concentrated near reliable freshwater sources, where Chumash activities
were also focused. Given Santa Cruz's rugged topography, land routes
connecting these places have remained mostly unchanged to this day.
The trails, paths, and roads built by historical ranchers likely follow in the
footsteps of Indigenous ones throughout the archipelago. These similarities and differences allow us to develop more nuanced understandings of
the legacies of ranching woven into the ecological fabric of the Channel
Islands (figure 6.5).

San Miguel Island is situated at the western end of the Northern
Channel Island chain; however, its reputation as harsh, windswept, and
foggy left it somewhat overlooked historically. Despite 12,000 years of
Chumash occupation, no Mexican citizen applied for a land grant during the Mexican Era. Consequently, when San Miguel became part of
the United States in 1850, it entered the public domain.[27] Mexican Era
squatters likely used the island for fishing, sea mammal hunting, and
other activities, but little is known of these activities in archaeological or
historical records. One of the only reports of the island during the early
19th century comes from Eugène Duflot de Mofras, a French naturalist
and explorer, who reported that San Miguel was used as a waypoint for
fur sealers to salt down their hides.

Historical accounts have left few records documenting when the
first sheep were brought to the island, but it was likely sometime prior
to 1850. George Nidever first established a large-scale sheep ranch
on San Miguel in the early 1850s. In his memoirs, Nidever described

purchasing the ranch from a man named Bruce, who ran a small sheep-grazing operation. Nidever and his sons, Mark and George, stocked the island with 45 sheep, 17 cattle, two hogs, and seven horses. After little more than a decade, the stock swelled to 6,000 sheep, 200 cattle, 100 hogs, and 32 horses, but was devastated by a severe 1863–1864 drought that resulted in the loss of 5,000 sheep, 180 cattle, several hogs, and 30 horses.[28] At the urging of his sons, who were weary of life on remote San Miguel, Nidever sold his ranching operation to the Mills brothers in 1870 for US$10,000.

Nidever's ranching efforts on San Miguel were brief compared to the nearly 80 years of sheep ranching that would follow, but his legacy left an indelible mark on the island. San Miguel is characterized by large sand dunes that cover much of the island, most of which were stabilized by native vegetation. Nidever allowed sheep to range across the island, and their grazing left vast tracks of the island denuded of plant cover, especially in the severe drought of 1863–1864. Heavy grazing destabilized the sand dunes, which blew across the island driven by strong northwesterly winds, and caused severe soil erosion. Eight years after leaving San Miguel, Nidever noted that the island was almost completely blanketed in blowing sand.

From 1870 to 1887, Hiram and Warren Mills, operating as the Pacific Wool Growing Company, grazed sheep on the island and shipped wool to mainland markets. The operation grew, but it is not clear how many sheep roamed the island. What is clear is that grazing caused continuing stress on island soils and vegetation. William Dall of the US Coast Survey wrote that "sheep crop every green thing within their reach," and Paul Schumacher described starving sheep in the 1870s and San Miguel as "a barren lump of sand."[29]

In 1887, William G. Waters, a former first lieutenant during the American Civil War, bought a half interest in San Miguel Island and its livestock and would spend the next 30 years living on the remote island. Waters's wife, Minnie Richardson Scott, kept a detailed diary, describing their toils to maintain a successful sheep ranch and productive garden. The Waterses planted nearly 50 acres of barley, grew vegetables, churned butter, constructed wire fencing, blasted a road from the harbor to the top of the island, and built a ranch complex that was eventually covered by blowing sands.

By the end of the 19th century, Waters took on several partners and filed to incorporate the San Miguel Island Company. Since San Miguel had never been part of any Mexican land grant and had no clear title of ownership, a series of court cases spanning years eventually determined that the US government owned the island. Waters's company was dissolved, but he continued ranching under a 1911 federal lease until he died in 1917.

Prior to his death, Waters subleased his ranching operation to mainland ranchers, Robert Brooks and J. R. Moore. They ran sheep and produced wool for another 30 years and made a variety of improvements, maintaining a wharf, shearing pens, a wool house, and a blacksmith shop and planting feed grasses across the island. Their sheep herds swelled to 4,000 but shrank significantly during drought years. Presumably, island soils and vegetation continued to suffer as introduced grasses such as Australian salt brush choked out native communities and blowing sands swirled across the island.

In 1929, needing help maintaining ranching operations on the island, Brooks enlisted the services of an army buddy, Herbert Steever Lester. Lester found life on San Miguel Island, far removed from the trappings of modern society, just the relief he needed from the shell shock he suffered in World War I. The 12 years Lester, his wife, Elizabeth, and their two children spent on the island is vividly recorded in Mrs. Lester's memoir, *The Legendary King of San Miguel*. Elizabeth detailed their spartan but idyllic time on the island, adding books, pictures, curtains, a fireplace, and other amenities to their sprawling "Rancho Rambouillet"—named after the island sheep and Herbert's favorite place in France—where they entertained guests with stories of island adventures in the "Killer Whale Bar" (figure 6.6). Stories of the Lester family were told in local Santa Barbara media and eventually in national outlets such as *Life* magazine.

Fame was short lived, however, and the Lesters' time on San Miguel came to a sudden and tragic end. In June 1942, with the US Navy threatening to take control of the island as a World War II coastal lookout station, Herbert took his own life. He was buried overlooking his favorite view on Harris Point, and within two weeks, his family had packed their belongings and left the island. Brooks hired one more island manager after Lester's death, but in 1948 the navy revoked his lease and ordered

Figure 6.6.   Aerial photograph of Rancho Rambouillet on San Miguel Island. Inset: The Lester family at their ranch home, overlooking Cuyler Harbor. *Source:* **open access images via islapedia.com.**

the removal of all sheep and other properties from the island. A century of ranching came to an abrupt end, and San Miguel was converted to a military training zone and bombing target range.

Anacapa Island followed a similar trajectory. No Mexican Era land grant was awarded for its three islets, leaving it in the public domain when the United States took over in 1848. Six years later, President Franklin Pierce issued an Executive Order reserving the island for lighthouse purposes. The first lighthouse was a makeshift metal skeleton on East Anacapa, and not until 1932 was the modern lighthouse, fog signal, and infrastructure completed on the eastern tip of East Anacapa.

Until documented ranching activities began in the early 20th century, we know little about historical period Anacapa Island except for occasional newspaper accounts, diaries and biographies, and historical maps, which hint at various clandestine activities occurring over the next half century. A logbook from the 1853 US Coast Survey, for example, described the remains of an old house on Middle Anacapa, most likely constructed by early fishermen or marine mammal hunters. H. Bay Webster, a seal hunter, operated on Anacapa for five years starting in 1890, and he described a lone structure on the island as a Chinese fishing shack in 1884. Newspaper accounts describe boaters visiting Anacapa in 1890 and stumbling upon a camp of Chinese abalone fishermen. Various colorful characters occupied the island, often as squatters, to fish, trap lobsters, or hunt bird eggs. There was even a brief gold rush on the island in the late 19th century, when prospectors claimed to have struck a "gold-bearing quartz," but riches never materialized.

Although the island was much smaller than the other three islands, ranching operations were eventually established on Anacapa. Sheep ranching began in the late 19th century, but the earliest surviving lease is dated 1902 and was awarded to Louis le Mesagner. Several hundred sheep grazed the island, centered on Middle Anacapa where they could be moved on and off along the northwest side at Shephard's Landing. With little water and delicate native vegetation, grazing quickly took a heavy toll on the landscape.

H. Bay Webster, the seal hunter, took over the lease in 1907 and briefly increased the herd to 600 animals. Poaching by fishermen and eagles, along with episodic drought, took their toll, but Webster and his family continued to operate out of Middle Anacapa for a decade, eking out a living through breeding and wool production. Webster's attempt to renew his lease was thwarted in 1917, when a notorious rumrunner, Ira K. Eaton, outbid him, likely motivated by securing an illegal liquor storage location on the island. By the 1930s, after three decades of grazing had stripped the island of much of its native vegetation, exotic grasses were introduced to help feed the hungry animals, but the lack of rain, forage, and fresh water for much of the year made ranching difficult. In 1938, Anacapa was designated a National Monument, and most of the sheep were removed from the island.

PROTECTING THE NATURAL AND CULTURAL TREASURES OF THE NORTHERN CHANNEL ISLANDS

By the 1930s, growing recognition by scientists and federal agencies of the unique history, flora, and fauna of the Channel Islands garnered attention at the highest levels of national government. On April 26, 1938, President Franklin D. Roosevelt designated Anacapa and Santa Barbara islands part of Channel Islands National Monument. Roosevelt made clear the islands' importance in the opening paragraph of his proclamation:

> Whereas certain public islands lying off the coast of Southern California contain fossils of Pleistocene elephants and ancient trees, and furnish noteworthy examples of ancient volcanism, deposition, and active sea erosion, and have situated thereon various other objects of geological and scientific interest.[30]

The NPS was tasked with protecting and managing the islands, including returning their landscapes to their "natural" condition. After a visit in 1946 by NPS chief landscape architect Thomas Vint, who was captivated by the diverse marine life and seascapes, President Harry S. Truman added one nautical mile offshore of Anacapa and Santa Barbara islands to the monument.

The transition of the islands from a national monument to a national park did not begin until 1961, when President John F. Kennedy addressed a special message to Congress arguing the importance of national parks and forests and imploring Congress to identify and establish additional shoreline parks. Through the 1960s and 1970s, several attempts were made to designate the Northern Channel Islands and Santa Barbara Island a national park or seashore, but these were stalled. Not until March 14, 1979, did Congressman Robert J. Lagomarsino successfully introduce a bill creating Channel Islands National Park. The House of Representatives passed the bill that summer, and the Senate followed suit in October. President Jimmy Carter signed it into law on March 5, 1980, establishing the islands of Anacapa, Santa Cruz, Santa Rosa, San Miguel, and Santa Barbara as Channel Islands National Park, with the US Navy continuing to own San Miguel even as it was managed by the NPS. In 2003, the State of California Fish and Game Commission established 13 Marine Protected Areas (MPAs) within the state waters of Channel Islands National Park. Three years later, the boundaries of these no fish zones were extended into federal waters of the Channel Islands Marine Sanctuary, and today 21 percent of park and sanctuary waters are protected by MPAs.

Although described as part of the park, Santa Rosa and Santa Cruz islands continued to be owned by private ranching families until the mid-1980s. In December 1986, the federal government reached an agreement to purchase Santa Rosa Island from Vail & Vickers, who gradually wound down their ranching and commercial hunting operations. The owner of the Santa Cruz Island Company, Carey Stanton, died in 1987, and his island property passed to The Nature Conservancy (TNC) for long-term preservation, protection, and restoration. The NPS purchased the eastern end of the island from the Gherini family in the 1990s, then in 2000 TNC transferred 8,500 acres of its property to the NPS. Today, the eastern 24 percent of Santa Cruz is part of Channel Islands National Park, while the remainder is TNC land. The two agencies work together to steward the resources of Santa Cruz Island. Their efforts have contributed to major conservation milestones on the Northern Channel Islands, including the successful removal of cattle, sheep, pigs, deer, elk, and other introduced animals, as well the reintroduction of bald eagles and the recovery of the island fox from the brink of extinction.

In chapter 7, we explore the future of the Northern Channel Islands. While the islands and their surrounding waters are overseen by different agencies, their managers and scientists are united in the ultimate goal of preserving, protecting, and restoring their precious natural and cultural resources, many of which occur nowhere else in the world. The islands are a biodiversity hot spot, where hikers and divers can see some of the rarest plants and animals on earth. And thousands of archaeological sites tell the story of some of the first peoples to arrive in the Americas and the perseverance, fortitude, and inventiveness of their descendants to survive and thrive for more than 13,000 years. As we shall see, the NPS and TNC are increasingly looking to the past to help understand the modern ecological composition of Channel Island land and seascapes and to guide plans to conserve island resources for future generations.

7

ISLANDS OF HOPE

Restoration and the Future

For decades, most scientists, historians, and museums viewed Native Americans as "natural" parts of the early American landscape. They were seen as passive actors who lived in relative harmony with the world around them, reacting to climatic changes and natural disasters in ways similar to other animals, with mobility, dietary shifts, and other behavioral adjustments. Native Americans altered the world around them, but not in significant or measurable ways. As anthropologist Eric Wolf put it, they were a "people without history."[1] Today, we recognize just how wrong these assumptions were.

Like people of any time and place, Native Americans were ecosystem engineers. They transformed environments to suit their needs, rituals, customs, and ideals. Their activities, from hunting, fishing, and gathering to building homes, villages, and ceremonial areas, had measurable impacts, positive and negative, on local plant and animal species. They transported and introduced wild and domestic plants and animals to novel environments, helping expand their range and initiating ecological changes. Their landscape transformation and hunting activities played key roles in driving some species to extinction. They used fire to tame wild landscapes and encourage the proliferation of economically important plants and animals. This strong environmental influence worked in tandem with diverse knowledge systems, trade and interaction spheres, and many other cultural practices. Ancient people's influence on past land and seascapes was pervasive and altered much of the "natural" world, but it went largely unnoticed by scientists and the public alike.

The reasons for this are complex. One that must not be overlooked is linked to the legacy of European colonialism. At the time of European "discovery," as colonial powers expanded around the globe, much of the world was viewed as *terra nullius*, land literally considered to belong to no one despite the presence of thousands or even millions of Indigenous people. Conquering these lands required only bravery, ingenuity, and some divine providence. For the American West, European explorers and Euro-American pioneers were driven by the belief that settling, civilizing, and taming the wilderness was their "manifest destiny." Native Americans were viewed as little more than another animal species, not fully exploiting the resources God gave them. They could be enslaved or swept aside (often violently) as the imperialist mind-set of Spanish, Mexican, and American governments strove for new lands and riches. For early California, the myths of the kindly Mission fathers, the romance of the Spanish rancho period, and the cowboy frontier still capture the imagination of Hollywood and the American public.

Such narratives allowed the individuals and institutions of European and American powers to justify their violence against Native American communities, stealing their lands and their freedom, erasing their histories, and, often, ending their lives. They also fueled a Western fascination with European discovery and valor that continues today—from an annual re-creation of Cabrillo's landing on San Miguel Island to the canonization of Father Junípero Serra by the Catholic Church, and a bicentennial celebration of Lewis and Clark's 1804–1805 Corps of Discovery Expedition that opened the untamed wilds of the American West to white settlement. Of course, these lands were not empty; they were occupied by hundreds of thousands of Indigenous Native Americans, who actively managed and shaped their land and seascapes for millennia.

We should note that ecosystem management is not a uniquely human trait. By felling trees and building dams, North American beavers (*Castor canadensis*) capture water from free-flowing creeks and construct fertile wetlands that provide food, shelter, and resources for a variety of plants and animals. When Europeans arrived in North America, as many as 250 million beaver ponds existed along the continent's waterways.[2] Fueled by colonialism and the emergence of global markets, however, intensive fur trapping began in the early 1600s, causing the numbers and geographic range of beavers to decline dramatically. Scientists only recently recognized that beaver ponds are hot spots of biodiversity that provide critical habitat for fish, moose, and other species; they also help prevent floods and recharge aquifers, and the organic sediments that settle in them store massive amounts of carbon. Biologists are now actively working to protect beaver populations and restore them to many landscapes where they once thrived. Even so, only about 15 million beavers live in North America today, a fraction of their historical abundance.

Given what we now know about the ecosystem engineering of beavers, it should be no surprise that Indigenous peoples had much more sophisticated and pervasive engineering practices based on traditional ecological knowledge (TEK). Imagine what we can learn about effective ecosystem management practices from the study of Indigenous people who lived relatively sustainably on the Channel Islands and the California mainland for millennia—especially working collaboratively with contemporary Native communities. For thousands of years before Europeans arrived in North America, Native Americans largely worked in concert with the natural world to shape the landscapes and seascapes they lived in. In the more than 500 years since Columbus, much of North America has been transformed by exploding human populations, commercial fishing, farming, and ranching; landscape modifications such as strip mining, dam building, and the construction of massive cities and urban sprawl; and the many other impacts of industrialization and globalization.

As we noted in chapter 1, one effective strategy to combat modern environmental impacts and help restore ecosystems to a more natural state is to consult deep historical datasets such as the archaeological record. The conservation and restoration goals of historical ecology are no easy fix, however, especially given the widespread destruction or degradation of archaeological sites from urban development, climate change, marine erosion, looting, and other factors. Archaeological sites along California's mainland coast have been hit especially hard by such destructive forces, but many sites on the Channel Islands remain relatively pristine.

   Charles Darwin and Alfred Russel Wallace, the fathers of evolutionary theory, first recognized the potential of islands for understanding the
deep history of evolution and ecological change. Ever since, islands have
been central to studies of evolution, biogeography, ecology, and human-
environmental interactions. Relatively isolated islands afford scientists
the ability to test theories about the past, present, and future of cultural
and ecological systems at scales smaller and more manageable than
continents.[3] The study of islands can help decode the complex interplay
between people and environmental change and provide a framework for
understanding human influences and impacts across time and space.[4]
Records of climate changes and anthropogenic impacts, extinctions of
plants and animals, landscape modifications, and much more are often
more clearly visible on island versus continental systems.[5]
   California's Northern Channel Islands are among the best places in
the world to study historical ecology and apply the lessons of the past to
help manage the future. The Channel Islands offer a deep human history, including some of the earliest evidence for maritime peoples in the
Americas. They were continuously occupied by the Chumash and their
ancestors for at least 13,000 years. The study of island archaeological
sites shows that over many millennia relatively small and mobile hunter-
gatherer-fishers established permanently occupied coastal villages, some
with hundreds of residents led by hereditary chiefs. They relied on the
bounty of the sea—shellfish, fish, sea mammals, and marine birds—for
their proteins and an abundance of terrestrial plants for carbohydrates.
They developed a complex network of island-mainland trade, facilitated
by *tomols* and a shell bead money produced primarily by Islanders. They
also strongly influenced island environments for millennia, managing
plant communities with fire; introducing dogs, foxes, and mice; disrupting marine mammal populations; enhancing and later depleting several
important shellfish species; and creating distinctive landforms at their
large mounded villages. These impacts were significant, but they led to
very few extinctions on the islands that can be directly linked to human
action.
   In contrast, after European settlement the rate and scale of human
environmental impacts increased exponentially, especially between the
late 18th and mid-20th centuries. After permanent Chumash occupation of the islands ended in the 1820s, European or Euro-American

settlers, sea otter and seal hunters, whalers, and commercial ranchers fundamentally transformed Channel Island ecosystems, terrestrial and marine. First and foremost, early European settlers introduced Old World diseases that devastated the Chumash and their neighbors. With no immunological resistance to smallpox, measles, typhoid, pneumonia, syphilis, and other infectious diseases, Indigenous people fell victim to a series of epidemics that swept through Native California communities, causing what Spanish conquistador Hernán Cortés described as "distressing deaths from . . . disease."[6] Even today, as humanity struggles with a modern global pandemic, the scale of the devastation is nearly impossible to comprehend, with estimates of mortality ranging as high as 90 percent.

Russian and Euro-American overseers, accompanied by Native Alaskan hunters, descended on the islands and harvested sea otters, seals, and sea lions by the thousands. Immigrant Chinese fishermen arrived in San Francisco during California's Gold Rush and built commercial fisheries, including a lucrative abalone shell and meat trade on the Channel Islands, by the mid-1850s. Wrecked merchant ships accidentally introduced invasive rats to three of the four Northern Channel Islands.[7] Introduced livestock, such as pigs, goats, sheep, cattle, and horses—along with other nonnative animals—rapidly overgrazed the islands during the 1800s and 1900s. Ranching operations during this period caused widespread erosion, the introduction and spread of exotic plants, and the destruction of native flora and fauna.[8] Military outposts were built on many of the islands starting in the 1930s, accelerating with World War II and the Cold War.

As management of the Northern Channel Islands shifted to the National Park Service (NPS), The Nature Conservancy (TNC), and the Channel Islands National Marine Sanctuary (CINMS), a variety of goals have been developed for island use, ranging from conservation to recreation to national defense. Each island serves a variety of purposes and will continue to do so long into the future. The primary conservation mission, however, is to build sustainable and resilient island ecosystems, which reflect a "natural" California as it was prior to European settlement. This is no easy task as the islands have undergone tremendous ecological changes over the millennia. From roughly 23,000 to 10,000 years ago, the northern islands were all connected into a single super-island, Santarosae, with a land area roughly three to four times that of the islands today. Since the last glacial period, natural climatic shifts have changed the flora and fauna of the islands significantly. Less than 500 years ago, thousands of Chumash people lived on the islands, regularly burning island landscapes and intensively harvesting resources on land and at sea. For island managers, there are key questions: What ecological baseline should be used to help guide restoration? How do we restore the islands to a "natural" state when ecological conditions have shifted so dramatically over the millennia, the result of both natural climate changes and human impacts before and after European contact? See figure 7.1.

Until recently, the management focus on the Northern Channel Islands has been on reversing the extensive and well-documented effects of the ranching era. After several decades of difficult and expensive work, NPS and TNC managers have removed most of the introduced herbivores, such as horses, pigs, sheep, cattle, deer, and elk, resulting in a gradual, complex, and increasingly dramatic recovery of island vegetation. This was a critical first step, but removing historically introduced species and expecting the islands to simply recover to a "natural" state is not enough. The challenge is to develop a set of conservation and management goals using what we know about the deep history of ecological change on the Northern Channel Islands. As we have demonstrated, the islands have been (and are) in a nearly constant state of flux, and human-caused climate change is now accelerating the pace of change.

Clearly, we cannot return the islands to a pre-human Pleistocene state, when mammoths roamed a landscape covered with much more extensive forests of cypress, pine, and Douglas fir trees. A more realistic target is to aim for a pre-European baseline, but thousands of Chumash people and their pet dogs lived on the islands just 250 years ago. They burned island landscapes, harvested shellfish by the millions, intensively fished kelp beds and pelagic waters, and hunted sea mammals and birds. Channel Island ecosystems were far healthier and more pristine under Chumash stewardship than they are today, but we cannot simply rewind the clock back to a seemingly idyllic ecological state.

There is no one solution to conservation management. Rather, archaeology, deep history, and historical ecology offer a view of how ecosystems have changed during thousands of years and the roles

Geological Transition: 20,000-12,000 years ago
Natural glacial/interglacial change, sea level rise, warmer, dryer environments, temperate-forest dominated to shrubland/grassland dominated vegetation

Prehistoric Transition: 12,000-200 years ago
Growing Native American populations, natural ecosystems transitioning to increasingly anthropogenic ecosystems, variable human impacts on marine and terrestrial ecosystems, introduction of dogs and foxes, and possible other plants and animals

Historical Transition: 200-40 years ago
European colonization resulting in dramatic socio-cultural change and Chumash displacement, intensive commerical fishing and ranching, major changes in vegetation types and endemic species, widespread introduction of domesticated and wild plants and animals

Recent Transition: 40 years ago - today
Concerted efforts to restore island ecosystems and build resilient systems, removal of non-native plants and animals, interdisciplinary research and restoration efforts focused on cooperative management strategies

Figure 7.1. The Northern Channel Islands have undergone tremendous environmental and cultural transitions over the last 20,000 years; all provide relevant information to contemporary conservation management decisions. *Source:* **open access images.**

people played in directing or influencing that change. The amazing geological, ecological, and human history of the Northern Channel Islands helps identify the historical range of variation and provides multiple perspectives for guiding conservation efforts. Deciding what we want the islands to look like and what services they should provide humans, other organisms, and the world is an inherently political debate. The voices of conservationists, Chumash descendants, scientists, fishermen, hikers, boaters, tourists, and other stakeholders all need to be heard. To successfully preserve, restore, and protect the islands, we must foster discussion and dialog between various stakeholders and increase scientific input in management decisions.

Despite the seemingly overwhelming environmental challenges we currently face, the Northern Channel Islands are islands of hope. In just a few decades, the NPS and TNC have eradicated numerous invasive animals and plants, planted native vegetation, and helped the islands recover in striking ways. Just four decades ago, archaeologists working on western San Miguel Island were asked to be careful not to step on the few plants struggling to take hold. Historical overgrazing had transformed the island into a sand-waste with large areas stripped of soil. Today, much of the island is covered in vegetation, and during the rainy season, island landscapes explode in a symphony of colorful native plants and wildflowers. TNC, NPS, and CINMS are well equipped to continue this impressive work, consulting with a variety of stakeholders about the future of the islands and their surrounding waters, monitoring the progress of restoration and recovery efforts, interpreting the remarkably important natural and human history of the islands for the public, and working with interdisciplinary scientists to integrate the lessons of deep history into current management plans (sidebar 7.1).

Protecting and Managing the Channel Island Cultural Resources by Kristin M. Hoppa, Channel Islands National Park Archaeologist

The Channel Islands National Park's cultural resources team works alongside Chumash tribal partners, other traditionally associated peoples, and research partners from museums and universities throughout the world to understand and protect the internationally significant archaeological resources on the Channel Islands. The significance of these resources is highlighted in the park's 1980 enabling legislation and remains at the forefront of park management today.

With more than 2,800 documented archaeological sites, our small park has much to manage. Guided by the National Park Service (NPS) Climate Change Response Program, we prioritize documentation of sites most vulnerable to the effects of climate change, including sea cliff retreat and sea level rise. We also recognize that the islands' archaeological record contains valuable information that can contribute to broader questions on how the environment, including the density and diversity of various plant and animal species, has changed since the arrival of humans more than 13,000 years ago. We work closely with our natural resources colleagues in interdisciplinary work to address these larger questions. All of this is done in the spirit of public stewardship, doing our best to understand and convey the stories these resources hold while protecting them for future generations.

NPS works closely with Chumash tribal partners in the stewardship of their ancestral homelands. To this end, we facilitate meaningful participation in archeological survey and documentation efforts, consult on park projects and planning efforts, and incorporate Chumash perspectives into public orientation, interpretive, and education programs. One recent example is a collaborative research effort highlighting Chumash place-names of park locations that will help recognize and celebrate Chumash history and heritage in lands now managed as a national park.

The future of the Northern Channel Islands is yet to be written, but the prospects for how best to guide their continued recovery are exciting. The archaeological and historical records left by the Chumash and other island occupants is helping us chart a path forward. Historical ecological research will continue to be critical to three interrelated conservation issues facing island managers: (1) setting terrestrial and marine ecosystem restoration goals; (2) protecting rare and endemic plants and animals; and (3) building resilient systems in the face of anthropogenic climate change.

SETTING TERRESTRIAL AND MARINE ECOSYSTEM RESTORATION GOALS

The primary goal of habitat restoration and management on land and at sea is to return Northern Channel Island ecosystems to pre-ranching conditions. When the ancestors of the Chumash first arrived, the islands were in a state of transition. A glimpse of this can be seen today at the caliche forest on San Miguel Island, where you can gaze upon a ghostly assemblage of the white, twisted stalks of trees and shrubs that died more than 10,000 years ago but were preserved by blowing sands, percolating rainwater, and dissolved seashells that created these limestone-like geological formations.

As populations on the islands slowly increased and the climate warmed after the last glacial ended around 11,700 years ago, conifer forests were largely replaced by coastal scrub, chaparral, and grasslands. Fires—some ignited by humans and some caused by drying conditions—burned more regularly during this transition.[9] For the next several millennia, many wetlands dried up, coastal sage scrub and chaparral covered hillslopes, and coastal lowlands were progressively lost to rising seas. As Chumash populations grew, intentional burning may have intensified, a tool used to increase the extent and productivity of grasslands and their important "root crops" by keeping chaparral and scrub vegetation at bay. The islands now contain diverse and productive mosaics of grassland, shrubland, and woodland. These changes were driven by a combination of natural environmental changes and growing human intervention and landscape management. During the last 3,500 years, when signs of increased sociopolitical complexity appear among the Chumash, charcoal densities increase in island geological deposits. Charred plant food remains from archaeological sites suggest that the Chumash shaped island vegetation communities for millennia through fire management, creating and tending grasslands where blue dicks and other edible plant foods thrived, providing an important dietary staple for Islanders.[10]

Today, with the removal of exotic grazing animals introduced during the ranching period, native vegetation and endemic plants are showing promising signs of recovery.[11] Soil erosion has slowed in many areas, and moisture from fog is once again being captured by taller and denser vegetation, a critical source of water in coastal California ecosystems.[12] Climate change is threatening island communities, however, including a reduction of annual precipitation from rain and fog, as well as higher risk of wildfire. Nonnative grasses, fennel, and other invasive plants are still widespread and abundant on the Northern Channel Islands, legacies of the ranching era that will be difficult to eradicate. Island managers, however, continue to work to control or eliminate nonnative species and to promote native species across the islands. In the near absence of fire, however, chaparral and scrub vegetation are rapidly crowding out many island grassland prairies that have existed for millennia. Here, too, archaeological research is providing important insights into past plant communities, and managers must decide how to best mediate the spread of these different "natural" landscapes.

There is also much we can learn about marine ecosystems from more than 10,000 years of Chumash hunting, gathering, and fishing in inter-tidal and nearshore kelp forest habitats. In the last 20 years, the collapse of global commercial fisheries has taken center stage in both the scientific literature and popular press. The combination of overfishing, climate change, pollution, and other problems has helped drive some of the world's most important commercial fisheries to the brink of collapse or beyond. Many fisheries scientists now view deep historical records as essential for creating management and recovery plans and rebuilding marine fisheries and ecosystems around the world.

Around the four Northern Channel Islands and Santa Barbara Island, CINMS and NPS protect 1,470 square miles of ocean, where critical aquatic species and sensitive habitats are monitored, managed, and given an opportunity to recover from decades of intensive commercial and sport fishing. Island archaeological sites can play a key role in helping scientists interpret the recovery of many marine species. For example, thousands of measurements from California mussel, red and black abalone, owl limpet, and black turban snail shells from island archaeological sites can track the sizes, densities, and distributions of these species in island waters for 10,000 years. The population dynamics of such shellfish species through deep time provide important context for their health and recovery today.

The relevance of the ancient past is most obvious when considering the history of abalone fishing in southern California waters. The historical Pacific abalone fishery was once a thriving part of the California economy, with commercial and sport landings peaking in the late 1950s. By the 1970s and 1980s, however, overfishing, expanding sea otter populations, and the appearance of Withering Syndrome (a deadly bacterial disease) took a dramatic toll on abalone populations. In 1997, a moratorium was placed on all red abalone fishing south of San Francisco Bay, leaving open only a highly regulated sport fishery in northern California. Red abalone was the last of California's abalone species to be closed to commercial and sport fishing, as a moratorium had been placed on black (*Haliotis cracherodii*), green (*Haliotis fulgens*), pink (*Haliotis corregata*), and white (*Haliotis sorenseni*) abalone by the California Fish and Game Commission in the early 1990s. Despite careful management, monitoring, and nearly two decades of closures, there has been little sign of improvement for most of California's abalone. This contrasts sharply with Island Chumash harvest, which was intensive and continuous for at least 12,000 years.

Red abalone may be the one bright spot for the recovery of the California abalones. Unlike California's other abalones, red abalone have expanded their numbers and range across much of coastal southern California, especially around the Northern Channel Islands. San Miguel Island has seen especially promising increases in red abalone densities, likely spurred by the strong upwelling and cold-water influx that made San Miguel waters the focus of commercial and recreational harvests before the 1997 closure. Commercial divers have lobbied for more than a decade for opening a small test fishery around San Miguel Island. The debate continues, entangled with deliberations over the expansion and potential reintroduction of sea otter populations.

When the deep history of red abalone fishing is considered, historical, archaeological, and paleoecological data suggest that the distribution and abundance of red abalone has varied in the Santa Barbara Channel through time. Roughly 8,000 years ago, archaeological data suggest that the Chumash reduced sea otter populations in local areas, either through direct hunting or competitive exclusion (keeping otters out of some areas due to human presence). Sea otters are voracious predators of abalone and other shellfish, and their population decline resulted in highly productive red abalone (and other shellfish) populations. Shellfish productivity was enhanced by the restructuring of marine food webs, with humans replacing sea otters as top shellfish predators. This pattern was especially true on San Miguel Island, where red abalone were available for millennia, regardless of fluctuations in local water temperatures. Red abalone were only abundant on the other islands during extended periods when sea surface temperatures were colder than normal. Thus, the distribution and abundance of red abalone fluctuated through time, including a historical resurgence when sea otters were extirpated from the Santa Barbara Channel during the 19th-century commercial fur trade.

The modern implications of these findings are vital for the continued survival of red abalone in the wild and the potential reestablishment of a California fishery. For millennia, San Miguel Island waters maintained intensive red abalone fisheries and were critical habitat for larval production and recruitment that fed the larger Santa Barbara Channel during regional cold-water intervals. The first signs of red abalone recovery in the Santa Barbara Channel should occur in San Miguel Island waters, but a better test of a Channel-wide recovery of red abalone is their re-population of island shorelines to the east, where ancient fisheries flourished during optimal climatic conditions and the modern fishery was robust but less productive.

If reestablishing a red abalone fishery in San Miguel waters too early may endanger their broader recovery, restoring sea otters to island waters too soon might do the same. The Island Chumash example suggests, however, that a sustainable red abalone fishery may be able to coexist with small numbers of sea otters in island waters. An archaeological history of abalone fishing on the Northern Channel Islands suggests that red abalone populations should be allowed to fully recover and sea otter populations controlled if we hope to re-create a sustainable fishery that began at least 12,000 years ago.

An even more straightforward application of deep history to modern management can be found with black abalone. Black abalone have shown some signs of recovery since they were listed as an endangered species in 2009, but their population expansion has been slower in the Santa Barbara Channel. Archaeological evidence and a historical ecological approach, however, may improve their prospects for recovery. Rather than relying solely on modern ecological surveys or historical catch records to identify suitable habitat, we have identified areas of Channel Island shorelines where ancient, historical, and modern fisheries were all exceptionally productive.[13] These areas are long-term "hot spots" for persistent black abalone survival prior to the overfishing and disease that led to the closure of commercial and sport fisheries. This information can help restoration biologists pinpoint potential places for releasing juvenile abalone into the wild, hoping that a founding population will take hold and spread to adjacent areas. Hot spots that supported intensive black abalone fisheries for millennia may contain the right mix of environmental conditions where such "outplanting" (transplanting abalones grown elsewhere) and recovery have the greatest chances of success.

A final example of the importance of deep history in modern management comes from some of the largest and most emblematic of the Channel Island mammals, seals and sea lions. Each year upward of 200,000 of these pinnipeds, including individuals from six different species, visit and/or breed on the Northern Channel Islands, one of the largest rookeries in the world. Sea mammal biologists, including Robert DeLong of the National Marine Fisheries Service, NPS, and other partners have worked diligently to protect and increase Channel Island pinniped populations since the federal Marine Mammal Protection Act was passed in 1972. Their recovery on the islands has been an enormous conservation success, with huge numbers of animals crowding island beaches and rocky shores in recent years. It has been so successful, in fact, that seals and sea lions hauling out on the Channel Islands are now destroying numerous archaeological sites ranging in age from nearly 10,000 years ago to historical times.

For a time, data from island archaeological sites suggested that the recovery of pinnipeds on the islands may not have followed a fully "natural" trajectory. Today, island beaches host tens of thousands of elephant seals, but just a few Guadalupe fur seals recently began to visit San Miguel Island. In most Middle and Late Holocene archaeological sites, however, the bones of Guadalupe fur seals are abundant, but those of elephant seals are very rare.[14] The marked differences between archaeological data and the modern distribution of pinnipeds on the Channel Islands raised questions about whether the recovery of these marine mammals was an ecological anomaly not representative of ancient baselines. Recent biochemical analysis of small marine mammal bone fragments from several Paleocoastal sites between about 12,000 and 9,000 years old may have helped solve this mystery, however, as they included higher percentages of elephant seal bones.[15] This suggests not only that the structure of pinniped populations on the islands may have been altered by both Chumash and Euro-American hunting but also that they may now be returning to something resembling their natural state prior to the arrival of humans. Further study is needed to confirm this, but once again archaeological data are contributing to a broader understanding of the dynamic interactions between humans and island ecosystems over millennia.

PROTECTING RARE AND ENDEMIC
ANIMALS AND PLANTS

A key goal of any national park or TNC preserve is conserving the area's animal and plant life and protecting biodiversity. Channel Islands National Park and TNC lands on Santa Cruz are no exceptions, as the islands contain some 271 endemic plant and 23 endemic terrestrial animals, some found nowhere else in the world. The patterns of endemism and community composition across the islands are complex and require an understanding of both natural and cultural histories and how the two are entangled.

When humans first arrived, the four northern islands were united as Santarosae, three to four times larger than the islands are today. Santarosae was also closer to the mainland, which facilitated colonization by plants, animals, and humans. When rising seas flooded island land bridges between 11,000 and 9000 years ago, roughly 70 percent of Santarosae was submerged, shrinking terrestrial habitat and isolating plants and animals on smaller islands. Columbian (*Mammuthus columbi*) and pygmy (*Mammuthus exilis*) mammoths lived on Santarosae until about the time humans arrived, but there is no direct evidence that humans killed or scavenged them. Currently, it appears that habitat loss and reduced food supply triggered by climate change and rising seas led to their demise.

The history of other Channel Island endemic mammals is more complex. Currently, the archipelago is home to 10 endemic island mammal subspecies, and one of these, the island fox, provides an example of how coupled natural-cultural influences shaped the evolutionary histories of Channel Island wildlife. The exact timing and mechanism of fox colonization of the Northern Channel Islands is still debated. Opinions range from an intentional human introduction of foxes to the islands, to a natural colonization event with mainland foxes (or a single pregnant female) arriving on Santarosae clinging to a vegetation raft after a storm, or a combination of the two.

Direct radiocarbon dating of "fossil" Pleistocene fox bones (once argued to be more than 15,000 years old) found no fox bones older than about 7,400 years, suggesting a relatively recent arrival for foxes, more than 5,000 years after humans settled the islands.[16] This work was followed by detailed genetic studies of island fox remains, which suggest a fox colonization as much as 9,500 years ago.[17] We believe Chumash ancestors probably transported foxes to the islands sometime in the Early Holocene. A combination of human selection and island isolation reduced their size over time, a process known as island dwarfism. Foxes may have arrived when most of the islands were still connected as Santarosae, and sea level rise may have further isolated island fox populations from one another, resulting in genetic differentiation across the three northern islands they currently occupy—Santa Cruz, Santa Rosa, and San Miguel.

The degree of genetic differentiation after colonization from island to island, however, is difficult to determine. While isolation on any given island may have led to distinct island fox populations, the Chumash likely transported foxes among the islands prehistorically as part of a trade network, creating a degree of genetic mixing, though this requires further research.[18] We know something similar happened as recently as the 19th century, as historical accounts describe ranchers occasionally moving foxes between the islands. Island ranchers like Herbert Lester on San Miguel kept foxes as pets, and one lived for a time in the research labs at the Santa Barbara Museum of Natural History.

Understanding this complex history took center stage in the late 1990s, when island fox populations catastrophically declined on the northern islands and managers feared they were headed for extinction. Subspecies from Santa Cruz, Santa Rosa, and San Miguel rapidly were added to the federal endangered species list and a massive influx of money and scientific expertise helped these populations make a spectacular recovery.[19] Biologists maintained distinct island fox populations as part of their captive breeding program during this crisis, not only to reduce the risk of parasites and pathogens but also because federal listing mandated that subspecies be recovered independently. The possible long-term effects of this population decline are currently unknown, and it is worrisome that two subspecies were reduced to merely 15 individuals. Moving forward, island managers must decide the most appropriate conservation plan and whether subspecies isolation remains important. Considering the evidence for prehistoric and historical movements of foxes between islands, modern island foxes may be more isolated now than they have been for the last 10,000 years.

Related to island foxes has been the application of archaeology and historical ecology to the recovery of one of America's most iconic species. Bald eagles once nested on all eight Channel Islands but disappeared from the archipelago in the mid-1900s due to extermination by ranchers and the buildup of DDT (dichloro-diphenyl-trichloroethane) in island food webs. Government agencies and TNC wanted to restore this iconic bird to the Channel Islands but were concerned doing so might adversely affect endangered or sensitive species, including the island fox. In the 1990s, fox populations on the northern islands were devastated by golden eagles, which had formerly been driven away by territorial bald eagles. By 2000, the few surviving foxes were trapped and placed in a captive breeding program. Did bald eagles once feed on island foxes, and, if so, would their reintroduction threaten the survival of the fox and the success of the multimillion-dollar effort to save them?

To find out, the NPS turned to a team of archaeologists and biologists in 2000 to study the contents of a historical eagle nest on San Miguel Island, known to have been used by bald eagles as recently as 1939. Erlandson worked with Channel Islands National Park archaeologist Don Morris, Santa Barbara Museum of Natural History biologist Paul Collins, and National Marine Fisheries Service biologist Robert DeLong to excavate the remnants of this large nest, which once stood 4–5 feet high but had collapsed into a pile of large sticks roughly 8 feet in diameter. The remnants were carefully taken apart and its contents collected by hand or by screening the sediment within, under, and around it.

Nearly 10,000 animal bones and marine shells were recovered, including thousands of fish and seabird bones, as well as much smaller amounts of shellfish, mammal, and reptile remains. Bones from just two island foxes were recovered, both very old individuals whose carcasses were probably scavenged by eagles after death.[20] Stable isotope analysis of bald eagle and prey remains from this nest and other sites also helped reconstruct diet and changing ecosystems.[21] The results documented the diet and ecology of bald eagles on the islands during a poorly known period of the 19th and early 20th century and gave a green light to bald eagle reintroduction. Since this initial work, a number of additional, more recent bald eagle nest sites have been excavated and analyzed on Santa Rosa, Santa Cruz, Santa Catalina, and Anacapa islands, as well as a barn owl nest site on Santa Barbara Island, providing great insight into the historical ecology of these species and broader island ecosystems. Today bald eagles and island foxes have made a remarkable recovery and are thriving once again on the Northern Channel Islands.

Historical ecology and archaeology are relevant for tracing the histories of even the smallest island mammals, the extinct giant island deer mouse (*Peromyscus nesodytes*). These creatures, which called Santarosae and the Northern Channel Islands home for more than 40,000 years, descended from a colonization by mainland deer mice long before human arrival. Unlike mammoths and other large mammal species that tend to shrink after reaching islands, rodents tend to grow larger on islands over the millennia. This evolutionary process resulted in a 30–35 percent increase in body size for the "giant" island deer mouse. Rising postglacial seas separated Santarosae's giant mouse populations, and in the midst of these biogeographic changes, Chumash ancestors probably accidentally introduced smaller mainland deer mice (*Peromyscus maniculatus*) to the islands as stowaways in their boats.[22] Through competition, habitat alteration, and possibly human introduction of dogs and foxes, the giant island deer mouse probably went extinct roughly 8,000 to 7,000 years ago.[23] Today, the contemporary deer mouse is considered an endemic species on the Northern Channel Islands, but its history is closely tied with human activities in the deep past, making their story even more complicated and interesting. Ultimately, the island fox and deer mouse stories further illuminate the deep interconnections between humans and Channel Island ecosystems, as well as the need for management strategies to integrate biological and cultural perspectives.

Managing the Northern Channel Islands' 138 endemic plant taxa also is best accomplished with a deep understanding of the natural-human interplay that created the present. Some endemic plants, such as island ironwood (*Lyonothamnus floribundus*), are Pleistocene holdovers that survived the warming and drying of the Holocene by sheltering in cool and moist microenvironments. Island scrub oaks are important species on several Channel Islands with a presence dating well into the Pleistocene. Recent genetic work suggests that the Chumash may have moved acorns/oaks between islands, however, and increased gene flow between separate island organisms.[24] The ancestors of other endemics thrived with the changing climatic conditions of the Holocene and opportunistically radiated into open niches and developed into new species or types as Ice Age climates ameliorated and low-lying coastal plains were drowned by rising seas. The result is a flora uniquely adapted to Northern Channel Island environments but potentially threatened by looming climate change.

It may seem that removing the grazing animals that wreaked havoc on native vegetation during the ranching period would allow endemic species to rapidly recover. Restoring these taxa is a much more complicated and difficult task,[25] however, and many endemic plants cannot effectively compete with other species in today's altered conditions. A passive recovery following the removal of exotic animals may help restore some natives, but others need more help. On Santa Rosa Island, a relict stand of Torrey pines (*Pinus torreyana*) is now expanding its range, and on Santa Cruz, island ironwoods (*Lyonothamnus floribundus*) and Bishop pines (*Pinus muricata*) are recovering (figure 7.2). Blue dicks (*Dipterostemon capitatus*), live-forevers (*Dudleya* spp.), and many other native

Figure 7.2. Photographs of Santa Rosa Island landscapes: (A) the Torrey Pine grove (*source:* open access image via islapedia.com); (B) rare island oaks (*source:* open access image via islapedia.com); and (C) grasslands dominated by historically introduced species (*source:* Todd J. Braje).

plants are also flourishing with little human intervention. For other species, more active management is required. On Santa Cruz Island, for example, hand pollination to increase seed output, establishment of new populations, and invasive plant control are all being employed to help struggling endemics recover.

As island plant communities recover, we cannot assume that landscapes are returning to pre-Spanish-contact conditions or a "natural" state. At least 10 endemic island plants were driven to extinction during historical times. Emerging research suggests that the Chumash may have introduced plants to the islands from the mainland. Add to this a long history of Native American landscape burning, management, and tending of useful wild plants, and the management of island plant communities becomes a more complicated and interesting task, one that will require reconstructing Holocene vegetation records with paleobotanical, pollen, and historical ecological studies.

BUILDING RESILIENT SYSTEMS IN THE FACE OF ANTHROPOGENIC CLIMATE CHANGE

Perhaps the biggest threat facing the Northern Channel Islands in decades to come is the risks posed by anthropogenic climate change. Future climate projections suggest that the accelerated pace of changes may create novel ecosystems and force managers to make unprecedented decisions without historical analogs.[26] Climate warming, shifts in the timing and intensity of precipitation, and declines in fog levels may heighten vulnerability of the archipelago's native species and communities.[27] Environmental conditions may change so quickly that some native plant and animal species may be unable to adapt to new habitats. The risks are especially high for species with limited dispersal ability, those unable to migrate to microenvironments where they can find refuge under rapidly changing environmental conditions.

Some impacts from anthropogenic climate change are already being felt in Channel Island ecosystems. Reproductively mature individuals are being lost, for example, and unusually high mortality rates have been recorded among young plants due to the reduction of fog cover.[28] Resource managers and biologists also are increasingly concerned that changes in precipitation and temperature for some endemic plant taxa will result in a failure to germinate and produce plentiful seeds.[29]

One of the challenges managers will face is sea level rise. Rising seas are nothing new for the islands, but coastlines have been relatively stable for the last 7,000 to 6,000 years. This means that plant and animal species have adapted to a set of fairly predictable and constant ecological communities and habitats for millennia, especially along island shorelines. This was not always the case, as rapidly rising seas between 18,000 and 7,000 years ago had important consequences for island flora and fauna, creating new habitats in some cases and eliminating others. As discussed in chapter 4, a productive estuary existed on eastern Santa Rosa Island from at least 11,000 to 6,000 years ago. Rapidly rising seas inundated the mouths of coastal drainages in the area. This estuary, where fresh and salt water mixed, was once home to a variety of shellfish that no longer occur on the islands; it also provided productive habitat for many bird species and the ancestors of the Chumash.

Some of the potential effects of accelerating sea level rise in the coming decades are difficult to forecast. Will the Abalone Rocks marsh once again be transformed into a productive estuary? Elsewhere, because of steep offshore bathymetry, relatively small amounts of land area are likely to be lost when compared to that of the terminal Pleistocene inundation. Marine erosion and sea cliff retreat will accelerate in many areas, however, threatening or destroying hundreds of significant archaeological sites created by the Chumash and their ancestors, Chinese fishermen, ranchers, rum-runners, and others. Coastal dune ecosystems, hot spots of biodiversity and endemism on the Channel Islands, could be severely affected if the rate of rise is too rapid for such habitat to "migrate" inland or for organisms to adapt. Many near-shore habitats, such as freshwater marshes, could be lost, reduced, or relocated. Plants and animals that rely on these habitats will be affected, including unique communities such as endemic dune insects, seabird nesting colonies, and rare plants. Sea level rise could also alter or destroy critical northern elephant seal rookery and haul-out sites on San Miguel and the other Channel Islands.

Ultimately, island managers and conservationists will need to predict how climate change in the coming decades is likely to affect the natural and cultural resources of the islands and develop strategies to mitigate threats and build resilient systems. Once again, archaeological and other deep time perspectives provide lessons of hope. Because so many of the archipelago's plants and animals have adapted and survived the dramatic changes of the Pleistocene and Holocene, there are many reasons to believe we can meet the challenges of the Anthropocene.

ISLANDS OF HOPE, ISLANDS OF CHANGE

The resilience of Northern Channel Island ecosystems and the remarkable recovery efforts of the NPS, TNC, National Marine Fisheries Service, and others all provide beacons of hope. Thirty years ago, the islands were a shadow of what they are today. Blue whales, fin whales, elephant seals, and many other marine mammals, once rare or endangered, frequent island waters once again. Pelicans, bald eagles, island foxes, and other iconic animals have recovered or been reintroduced to the islands. Removal of introduced cattle, sheep, and other exotic herbivores—along with careful management and strategic planning—has helped many native plants and animals thrive once more. During your next visit to the islands, you are likely to see a diverse array of seabirds flying over brilliant azure and turquoise waters, stunning vistas of wildflowers, and a natural beauty that is difficult to match. As we have shown, however, these beautiful land and seascapes have long histories deeply intertwined with amazing geological forces, climate changes, and the cultural dynamism of a proud Indigenous people who lived on the islands for more than 13,000 years. The Chumash and their ancestors left behind an internationally significant record of human and environmental interaction, a history recorded in archaeological sites, ethnohistoric accounts, traditional knowledge, and a continuing revitalization of their deep ties to the Channel Islands and the broader region. That history is still recognized in Chumash place-names such as Malibu (*Humaliwo*), Lompoc (*Lompo'*), Anacapa (*'Anyapax*), *Limuw* (Santa Cruz Island), *Wima* (Santa Rosa Island), *Tuqan* (San Miguel Island), and many more.

Protecting and managing the islands will take cooperative and focused efforts by resource managers, Chumash descendants, scientists, political leaders, and other advocates and stakeholders. Central among these should be collaborative efforts with the Chumash community, whose ancestors were island stewards for millennia. Chumash traditional histories of their people and the islands have been passed down through countless generations, and their traditional knowledge functions as a library of ecological understandings. Protected areas and national parks have been created, in many cases, by taking land from Indigenous communities and excluding them from conservation programs. For too long and all too often, their histories and viewpoints were ignored or dismissed.

Channel Islands National Park, TNC, and Channel Islands National Marine Sanctuary are all actively working with Chumash representatives as key players in the development of management plans. This includes careful consultation in scientific and restoration programs, connecting Chumash youth with their ancestral lands and history, and authentically communicating the Chumash history and stories of their island homes. One particularly powerful tradition that has been revitalized is what has become an annual *tomol* crossing between the mainland and the islands organized by the Chumash Maritime Association and other tribal groups (figure 7.3).

Figure 7.3. Photograph from the 2015 Chumash *tomol* crossing from Channel Islands Harbor to Santa Cruz Island. Twenty-five "pullers" rotated into the six-person canoe and were supported by the Channel Islands Marine Sanctuary vessel *Shearwater*. Source: open access image via commons.wikimedia.org.

Using traditional knowledge passed down through generations and recorded in ethnohistoric accounts told by Chumash elder Fernando Librado Kitsepawit, the Chumash Maritime Association built a 26-foot-long redwood plank canoe named *'Elye'wun*, the Chumash word for swordfish. On September 8, 2001, they paddled *'Elye'wun* from the mainland to Santa Cruz Island, where they were greeted on the beach by more than 150 family and friends. Three years later, another successful crossing was made, a 21-mile voyage that took more than 10 hours. This time more than 200 friends and family celebrated their arrival at the Chumash village of *Swaxil*, at Scorpion Harbor on *Limuw*. The *tomol* crossing continues today and is just one of the ways that the links between Chumash ancestors and modern Chumash communities is renewed, celebrated, and strengthened.

One of the most pressing challenges facing us, however, is the rapid loss of Chumash cultural heritage sites to erosion and other natural and cultural processes that are actively destroying archaeological sites. Every year, every month, and every day more and more archaeological resources erode into the sea and are lost to all, a process that is accelerating due to anthropogenic climate change and rising seas. These sites tell the stories of the deep history of the Chumash on the islands, but they are also archives of what the island ecosystems once looked like. The invaluable information they contain can provide road maps to help us reimagine island land and seascapes and build effective and resilient island ecosystems.

If the future of the Channel Islands is hopeful, it also remains to be written. Island managers will decide how to steer recovery efforts and help shape the future of island ecosystems. Their decisions will be guided, however, by lessons from the deep past and the voices and actions of people like you. The Chumash and their ancestors helped shape the ecology of the islands for more than 10 millennia, and now scientists and managers are using the archaeological, ethnographic, and oral histories they left behind to better understand why the Channel Islands look the way they do today and what they should look like in the future. Please join us and thousands of Chumash descendants in being, or becoming, a responsible steward and advocate for this amazing archipelago and its remarkable natural and cultural resources.

NOTES

CHAPTER I

1. Warren L. Wagner, Derral R. Herbst, and S. H. Sohmer, *Manual of the Flowering Plants of Hawai'i*, rev. ed., 2 vols., Bernice Pauahi Bishop Museum Special Publication (Honolulu: University of Hawai'i Press, 1999).

2. Daniel Pauly, "Anecdotes and the Shifting Baseline Syndrome of Fisheries," *Trends in Ecology and Evolution* 10, no. 10 (1995): 430.

3. Pauly, "Anecdotes and the Shifting Baseline Syndrome of Fisheries," 430.

4. Carl Safina, *Song for the Blue Ocean: Encounters along the World's Coasts and beneath the Seas* (New York: Holt Paperbacks, 1999); Carl Safina, *Eye of the Albatross: Visions of Hope and Survival* (New York: Holt Paperbacks, 2003).

5. Carl Safina, "A Shoreline Remembrance," in *Shifting Baselines: The Past and the Future of Ocean Fisheries*, ed. Jeremy B. C. Jackson, Karen E. Alexander, and Enric Sala, 13–19 (Washington, DC: Island Press, 2011).

6. Heike K. Lotze and Loren McClenachan, "Marine Historical Ecology: Informing the Future by Learning from the Past," in *Marine Community Ecology and Conservation*, ed. Mark Bertness, John Bruno, Brian Silliam, and Jay Stachowicz, 165–200 (Oxford, UK: Sinauer Associates, 2013).

7. Péter Szabó, "Historical Ecology: Past, Present, and Future," *Biological Reviews* 90, no. 4 (2015): 997–1014.

CHAPTER 2

1. Deborah R. Harden, *California Geology*, 2nd ed. (Upper Saddle River, NJ: Pearson Prentice Hall, 2004).

2. Robert M. Norris, *The Geology and Landscape of Santa Barbara County, California and Its Offshore Islands* (Santa Barbara, CA: Santa Barbara Museum of Natural History, 2003).

3. Daniel R. Muhs, Kathleen R. Simmons, Lindsey T. Groves, John P. McGeehin, R. Randall Schumann, and Larry D. Agenbroad, "Late Quaternary Sea-Level History and the Antiquity of Mammoths (*Mammuthus exilis* and *Mammuthus columbi*), Channel Islands National Park, California, USA," *Quaternary Research* 83, no. 3 (2015): 502–21.

4. Jeffery S. Pigati, Daniel R. Muhs, and John P. McGeehin, "On the Importance of Stratigraphic Control for Vertebrate Fossil Sites in Channel Islands National Park, California, USA: Examples from New *Mammuthus* Finds on San Miguel Island," *Quaternary International* 443 (Part A) (2017): 129–39.

5. John R. Johnson, Thomas W. Stafford Jr., Henry O. Ajie, and Don P. Morris, "Arlington Springs Revisited," in *Proceedings of the Fifth California Islands Symposium*, ed. David R. Browne, Kathryn L. Mitchell, and Henry W. Chaney (Santa Barbara, CA Santa Barbara Museum of Natural History, 2002), 541–45.

6. Jon M. Erlandson, Torben C. Rick, Todd J. Braje, Molly Casperson, Brendan Culleton, Brian Fulfrost, Tracy Garcia, et al., "Paleoindian Seafaring, Maritime Technologies, and Coastal Foraging on California's Channel Islands," *Science* 331, no. 6021 (2011): 1181–85.

7. Todd J. Braje, Tom D. Dillehay, Jon M. Erlandson, Richard G. Klein, and Torben C. Rick, "Finding the First Americans," *Science* 358, no. 6363 (2017): 592–94.

8. Leslie Reeder-Myers, Jon M. Erlandson, Daniel R. Muhs, and Torben C. Rick, "Sea Level, Paleogeography, and Archeology on California's Northern Channel Islands," *Quaternary Research* 83, no. 2 (2015): 263–72.

9. Alexis M. Mychajliw, Torben C. Rick, Nihan D. Dagtas, Jon M. Erlandson, Brendan J. Culleton, Douglas J. Kennett, Michael Buckley, and Courtney A. Hofman, "Late Pleistocene Translocation of a Short-Faced Bear to the California Channel Islands: Insights from Biogeographic Problem-Solving," *Nature Scientific Reports* 10 (2020): 15172.

10. Allan A. Schoenherr, C. Robert Feldmeth, and Michael J. Emerson, *Natural History of the Islands of California* (Berkeley: University of California Press, 1999).

11. Linda Heusser, "Pollen in Santa Barbara Basin, California: A 12,000-Yr Record," *Geological Society of America Bulletin* 89, no. 5 (1978): 673–78.

12. Phil C. Orr, *Prehistory of Santa Rosa Island* (Santa Barbara, CA: Santa Barbara Museum of Natural History, 1968); Ralph W. Chaney and Herbert L. Mason, *A Pleistocene Flora from Santa Cruz Island, California* (New York: Carnegie Institution, 1930).

13. Nicole L. Boivin, Melinda A. Zeder, Dorian Q. Fuller, Alison Crowther, Greger Larson, Jon M. Erlandson, Tim Denham, and Michael D. Petraglia, "Ecological Consequences of Human Niche Construction: Examining Long-Term Anthropogenic Shaping of Global Species Distributions," *Proceedings of the National Academy of Sciences USA* 113, no. 23 (2016): 6388–96; Jon M. Erlandson and Todd J. Braje, eds., "When Humans Dominated Earth: Archeological Perspectives on the Anthropocene," special issue, *Anthropocene* 4 (2013): 1–125.

14. Brian P. Kinlan, Michael H. Graham, and Jon M. Erlandson, "Late Quaternary Changes in the Size, Shape, and Isolation of the California Islands: Ecological and Anthropological Implications," in *Proceedings of the Sixth California Islands Symposium*, ed. D. K. Garcelon and C. A. Schwemm (Arcata, CA: Institute for Wildlife Studies & National Park Service, 2005), 119–30.

15. Leslie Reeder-Myers, Jon M. Erlandson, Daniel R. Muhs, and Torben C. Rick, "Sea Level, Paleogeography, and Archeology on California's Northern Channel Islands," *Quaternary Research* 83, no. 2 (2015): 263–72.

16. Kristina Gill, "10,000 Years of Geophyte Use among the Island Chumash of the Northern Channel Islands," *Fremontia* 44, no. 3 (2016): 34–38.

CHAPTER 3

1. Jon M. Erlandson, Douglas J. Kennett, B. Lynn Ingram, Daniel A. Guthrie, Don P. Morris, Mark A. Tveskov, G. James West, and Phillip L. Walker, "An Archaeological and Paleontological Chronology for Daisy Cave (CA-SMI-261), San Miguel Island, California," *Radiocarbon* 38, no. 2 (1996): 355–73.

2. K. R. Fladmark, "Routes: Alternative Migration Corridors for Early Man in North America," *American Antiquity* 44, no. 1 (1979): 55–69.

3. Todd J. Braje, Jon M. Erlandson, Torben C. Rick, Loren Davis, Tom Dillehay, Daryl W. Fedje, Duane Froese, Amy Gusick, Quentin Mackie, Duncan McLaren, Bonnie Pitblado, Jennifer Raff, Leslie Reeder-Myers, and Michael R. Waters, "Fladmark + 40: What Have We Learned about a Potential

Pacific Coast Peopling of the Americas?" *American Antiquity* 85, no. 1 (2020): 1–21.

4. Braje et al., "Fladmark + 40."

5. Jon M. Erlandson, "Anatomically Modern Humans, Maritime Voyaging, and the Pleistocene Colonization of the Americas," in *The First Americans: The Pleistocene Colonization of the New World*, ed. Nina G. Jablonski (San Francisco: California Academy of Sciences, 2002), 59–92.

6. Tom D. Dillehay, *Monte Verde: A Late Pleistocene Settlement in Chile*, vol. 2, *The Archaeological Context* (Washington, DC: Smithsonian Institution Press, 1997).

7. T. D. Dillehay, C. Ramirez, M. Pino, M. B. Collins, J. Rossen, and J. D. Pino-Navarro, "Monte Verde: Seaweed, Food, Medicine, and the Peopling of South America," *Science* 320, no. 5877 (2008): 784–86.

8. Jon M. Erlandson, Michael H. Graham, Bruce J. Bourque, Debra Corbett, James A. Estes, and Robert S. Steneck, "The Kelp Highway Hypothesis: Marine Ecology, the Coastal Migration Theory, and the Peopling of the Americas," *Journal of Island and Coastal Archaeology* 2, no. 2 (2007): 161–74.

9. Jon M. Erlandson, Todd J. Braje, Kristina M. Gill, and Michael H. Graham, "Ecology of the Kelp Highway: Did Marine Resources Facilitate Human Dispersal from Northeast Asia to the Americas?" *Journal of Island and Coastal Archaeology* 10, no. 3 (2015): 392–411.

10. Amy E. Gusick and Jon M. Erlandson, "Paleocoastal Landscapes, Marginality, and Early Human Settlement of the California Islands," in *An Archaeology of Abundance: Reevaluating the Marginality of California's Islands*, ed. Kristina M. Gill, Mikael Fauvelle, and Jon M. Erlandson (Gainesville: University Press of Florida, 2019), 59–97.

11. Phil C. Orr, *Prehistory of Santa Rosa Island* (Santa Barbara, CA: Santa Barbara Museum of Natural History, 1968).

12. Kristina M. Gill, Jon M. Erlandson, Ken Niessen, Kristin M. Hoppa, and Dustin Merrick, "Where Carbohydrates Were Key: Reassessing the Marginality of Terrestrial Plant Resources on California's Islands," in *An Archaeology of Abundance: Reevaluating the Marginality of California's Islands*, ed. Kristina Gill, Mikael Fauvelle, and Jon M. Erlandson (Gainesville: University Press of Florida, 2019), 98–134.

13. George G. Heye, *Certain Artifacts from San Miguel Island, California* (New York: Museum of the American Indian, Heye Foundation, 1921).

14. Gabriel M. Sanchez, Jon M. Erlandson, and Nicholas Tripcevich, "Quantifying the Association of Chipped Stone Crescents with Wetlands and Paleo-Shorelines of Western North America," *North American Archaeologist* 38, no. 2 (2017): 107–37.

15. Torben C. Rick, Jon M. Erlandson, and René L. Vellanoweth, "Paleo-coastal Marine Fishing on the Pacific Coast of the Americas: Perspectives from Daisy Cave, California," *American Antiquity* 66, no. 4 (2001): 595–613.

16. Thomas J. Connolly, Jon M. Erlandson, and Susan E. Norris, "Early Holocene Basketry and Cordage from Daisy Cave San Miguel Island, California," *American Antiquity* 60, no. 2 (1995): 309–18; René L. Vellanoweth, Melissa R. Lambright, Jon M. Erlandson, and Torben C. Rick, "Early New World Maritime Technologies: Sea Grass Cordage, Shell Beads, and a Bone Tool from Cave of the Chimneys, San Miguel Island, California, USA," *Journal of Archaeological Science* 30, no. 9 (2003): 1161–73.

17. Jon M. Erlandson, *Early Hunter-Gatherers of the California Coast* (New York: Plenum, 1994).

18. Seetha N. Reddy and Jon M. Erlandson, "Macrobotanical Food Remains from a Trans-Holocene Sequence at Daisy Cave (CA-SMI-261), San Miguel Island, California," *Journal of Archaeological Science* 39, no. 1 (2012): 33–40.

19. Gill et al., "Where Carbohydrates Were Key."

20. Jon M. Erlandson, Torben C. Rick, Todd J. Braje, Molly Casperson, Brendan Culleton, Brian Fulfrost, Tracy Garcia, et al., "Paleoindian Seafaring, Maritime Technologies, and Coastal Foraging on California's Channel Islands," *Science* 331, no. 6021 (2011): 1181–85.

21. Courtney A. Hofman, Torben C. Rick, Jon M. Erlandson, Leslie Reeder-Myers, Andreanna J. Welch, and Michael Buckley, "Collagen Fingerprinting and the Earliest Marine Mammal Hunting in North America," *Scientific Reports* 8, no. 1 (2018): 1–6.

22. Braje et al., "Fladmark + 40."

CHAPTER 4

1. Jon M. Erlandson, Torben C. Rick, Amira F. Ainis, Kristina M. Gill, Nicholas P. Jew, and Leslie A. Reeder-Myers, "Shellfish, Geophytes, and Sedentism on Early Holocene Santa Rosa Island, Alta California, USA," *Journal of Island and Coastal Archaeology* 15, no. 4 (2020): 504–24.

2. Lynn H. Gamble, "Feasting, Ritual Practices, Social Memory, and Persistent Places: New Interpretations of Shell Mounds in Southern California," *American Antiquity* 82, no. 3 (2017): 427–51.

3. Michael A. Glassow, "Chronology of Red Abalone Middens on Santa Cruz Island, California, and Evidence for Subsistence and Settlement Change," *American Antiquity* 80, no. 4 (2015): 745–59.

4. Douglas J. Kennett, *The Island Chumash: Behavioral Ecology of a Maritime Society* (Berkeley: University of California Press, 2005).

5. Todd J. Braje, Jon M. Erlandson, Torben C. Rick, Paul K. Dayton, and Marco B. A. Hatch, "Fishing from Past to Present: Continuity and Resilience of Red Abalone Fisheries on the Channel Islands, California," *Ecological Applications* 19, no. 4 (2009): 906–19.

6. Susan C. Kuzminsky, Jon M. Erlandson, and Tatiana Xifara, "External Auditory Exostoses and Its Relationship to Prehistoric Abalone Harvesting on Santa Rosa Island, California," *International Journal of Osteoarchaeology* 26, no. 6 (2016): 1014–23.

7. Charles A. Simenstad, James A. Estes, and Karl W. Kenyon, "Aleuts, Sea Otters, and Alternate Stable-State Communities," *Science* 200, no. 4340 (1978): 403–11.

8. Jon M. Erlandson, Torben C. Rick, James A. Estes, Michael H. Graham, Todd J. Braje, and René L. Vellanoweth, "Sea Otters, Shellfish, and Humans: 10,000 Years of Ecological Interaction on San Miguel Island, California," in *Proceedings of the Sixth California Islands Symposium*, ed. D. K. Garcelon and C. A. Schwemm (Arcata, CA: Institute for Wildlife Studies & National Park Service, 2005), 9–21.

9. Jon M. Erlandson, *Early Hunter-Gatherers of the California Coast* (New York: Plenum Press, 1994).

10. R. Scott Anderson, Scott Starratt, Benata M. Brunner Jass, and Nicholas Pinter, "Fire and Vegetation History on Santa Rosa Island, Channel Islands, and Long-Term Environmental Change in Southern California," *Journal of Quaternary Science* 25, no. 5 (2010): 782–97.

11. Torben C. Rick, Phillip L. Walker, Lauren M. Willis, Anna C. Noah, Jon M. Erlandson, René L. Vellanoweth, Todd J. Braje, and Douglas J. Kennett, "Dogs, Humans and Island Ecosystems: The Distribution, Antiquity and Ecology of Domestic Dogs (*Canis familiaris*) on California's Channel Islands, USA," *Holocene* 18, no. 7 (2008): 1077–87.

CHAPTER 5

1. John Johnson, "Chumash Population History," in *Cultural Affiliation and Lineal Descent of Chumash Peoples in the Channel Islands and Santa Monica Mountains*, ed. S. McLendon and J. R. Johnson (Washington, DC: Archaeology and Ethnography Program, National Park Service, 1999), 93–130.

2. John Johnson, "Ethnographic Reflections of Cruzeño Chumash Society," in *The Origins of a Pacific Coast Chiefdom: The Chumash of the Channel Islands*, ed. J. E. Arnold (Salt Lake City: University of Utah Press, 2001), 53–70.

3. Johnson, "Ethnographic Reflections of Cruzeño Chumash Society"; Thomas C. Blackburn, ed., *December's Child: A Book of Chumash Oral Narratives* (Berkeley: University of California Press, 1975); Travis Hudson and Ernest Underhay, *Crystals in the Sky: An Intellectual Odyssey Involving Chumash Astronomy, Cosmology and Rock Art*, Anthropological Papers 10 (Menlo Park, CA: Ballena Press, 1978).

4. Torben Rick, *The Archaeology and Historical Ecology of Late Holocene San Miguel Island* (Los Angeles: Cotsen Institute of Archaeology, 2007).

5. Jennifer E. Perry, "Quarries and Microblades: Trends in Prehistoric Land and Resource Use on Eastern Santa Cruz Island," in *Foundations of Chumash Complexity*, ed. J. E. Arnold (Los Angeles: Cotsen Institute of Archaeology, 2004), 113–32.

6. Torben C. Rick and Leslie A. Reeder-Myers, *Deception Island: Archaeology of 'Anyapax, Anacapa Island, California* (Washington, DC: Smithsonian Scholarly Press, 2018).

7. Douglas J. Kennett, Bruce Winterhalder, Jacob Bartruff, and Jon M. Erlandson, "An Ecological Model for the Emergence of Institutionalized Social Hierarchies on California's Northern Channel Islands," in *Pattern and Process in Cultural Evolution*, ed. S. Sheenan (Berkeley: University of California Press, 2009), 297–314; Christopher S. Jazwa, Douglas J. Kennett, Bruce Winterhalder, and Terry L. Joslin, "Territoriality and the Rise of Despotic Social Organization on Western Santa Rosa Island, California," *Quaternary International* 518 (2019): 41–56.

8. Douglas J. Kennett, *The Island Chumash: Behavioral Ecology of a Maritime Society* (Berkeley: University of California Press, 2005); John R. Johnson and Sally McLendon, "The Social History of Native Islanders Following Missionization," in *Proceedings of the Fifth California Islands Symposium*, ed. D. Browne, K. Mitchell, and H. Chaney (Santa Barbara, CA: Santa Barbara Museum of Natural History, 2000), 646–53.

9. Elizabeth A. Sutton, "Household and Community Organization at *Nimatlala*, an Island Chumash Village on *Limuw* (Santa Cruz Island), California" (PhD diss., University of California at Santa Barbara, 2014).

10. Jeanne E. Arnold, "Complex Hunter-Gatherer-Fishers of Prehistoric California: Chiefs, Specialists, and Marine Adaptations of the Channel Islands," *American Antiquity* 57, no. 1 (1992): 60–84.

11. Douglas J. Kennett and James P. Kennett, "Competitive and Cooperative Responses to Climatic Instability in Coastal Southern California," *American Antiquity* 65, no. 2 (2000): 379–95.

12. Jon M. Erlandson and Torben C. Rick, "Late Holocene Cultural Developments along the Santa Barbara Coast," in *Catalysts to Complexity: The Late Holocene on the California Coast*, ed. J. M. Erlandson and T. L. Jones (Los Angeles: Cotsen Institute of Archaeology, 2002), 166–82.

13. Travis Hudson, Janice Timbrook, and Melissa Rempe, eds., *Tomol: Chumash Watercraft as Described in the Ethnographic Notes of John P. Harrington*, Anthropological Papers 9 (Menlo Park, CA: Ballena Press, 1978).

14. Lynn H. Gamble, "Archaeological Evidence for the Origin of the Plank Canoe in North America," *American Antiquity* 67, no. 2 (2002): 301–15.

15. Demorest Davenport, John R. Johnson, and Jan Timbrook, "The Chumash and the Swordfish," *Antiquity* 67 (1993): 257–72.

16. Julienne Bernard, "Status and the Swordfish: The Origins of Large-Species Fishing among the Chumash," in *Foundations of Chumash Complexity*, ed. J. E. Arnold (Los Angeles: Cotsen Institute of Archaeology, 2004), 25–52.

17. Douglas J. Kennett, Patricia M. Lambert, John R. Johnson, and Brendan J. Culleton, "Sociopolitical Effects of Bow and Arrow Technology in Prehistoric Coastal California," *Evolutionary Anthropology* 22 (2013): 124–32.

18. Arnold, "Complex Hunter-Gatherer-Fishers of Prehistoric California."

19. Kennett, *The Island Chumash.*

20. Jon M. Erlandson, Torben C. Rick, Todd J. Braje, Alexis Steinberg, and René Vellanoweth, "Human Impacts on Ancient Shellfish: A 10,000-Year Record from San Miguel Island, California," *Journal of Archaeological Science* 35, no. 8 (2008): 2144–52.

21. Patricia M. Lambert and Phillip L. Walker, "Physical Anthropological Evidence for the Evolution of Social Complexity in Coastal Southern California," *Antiquity* 65 (1991): 963–73.

22. Todd J. Braje, Torben C. Rick, Paul Szpak, Seth D. Newsome, Joseph M. McCain, Emma A. Elliott Smith, Michael Glassow, and Scott L. Hamilton, "Historical Ecology and the Conservation of Large, Hermaphroditic Fishes in Pacific Coast Kelp Forest Ecosystems," *Science Advances* 3, no. 2 (2017): e1601759.

23. Daniel Pauly, Villy Christensen, Johanne Dalsgaard, Rainer Froese, and Francisco Torres Jr., "Fishing down Marine Food Webs," *Science* 279, no. 5352 (1998): 860–63.

24. Jon M. Erlandson, Torben C. Rick, and Todd J. Braje, "Fishing up the Food Web? 12,000 Years of Maritime Subsistence and Adaptive Adjustments on California's Channel Islands," *Pacific Science* 63, no. 4 (2009): 711–24.

25. Daniel A. Guthrie, "New Information on the Prehistoric Fauna of San Miguel Island, California," in *Third California Islands Symposium, Recent Advances in Research on the California Islands*, ed. F. G. Hochberg (Santa Barbara, CA: Santa Barbara Museum of Natural History, 1993), 405–16.

26. Kristina M. Gill and Kristin M. Hoppa, "Evidence for an Island Chumash Geophyte-Based Subsistence Economy on the Northern Channel Islands," *Journal of California and Great Basin Anthropology* 36, no. 1 (2016): 51–71.

27. Kristina M. Gill, "10,000 Years of Geophyte Use among the Island Chumash of the Northern Channel Islands," *Fremontia* 44, no 3 (2016): 34–38.

28. R. Scott Anderson, Scott Starratt, Benata M. Brunner Jass, and Nicholas Pinter, "Fire and Vegetation History on Santa Rosa Island, Channel Islands, and Long-Term Environmental Change in Southern California," *Journal of Quaternary Science* 25, no. 5 (2010): 782–97.

29. Johnson, "Ethnographic Reflections of Cruzeño Chumash Society."

30. David W. Robinson, Kelly Brown, Moira McMenemy, Lynn Dennany, et al., "Datura Quids at Pinwheel Cave, California, Provide Unambiguous Confirmation of the Ingestion of Hallucinogens at a Rock Art Site," *Proceedings of the National Academy of Sciences of the United States of America* 117, no. 49 (2020): 31026-37.

31. Jennifer Perry, "The Archaeology of Ritual on the Channel Islands," in *California's Channel Islands: The Archaeology of Human Environment Interactions*, ed. C. S. Jazwa and J. E. Perry (Salt Lake City: University of Utah Press, 2013), 137–55.

32. Jennifer Perry, "The Archaeology of Ritual on the Channel Islands," in *California's Channel Islands: The Archaeology of Human Environment Interactions*, ed. C. S. Jazwa and J. E. Perry (Salt Lake City: University of Utah Press, 2013), 137–55.

33. Perry, "The Archaeology of Ritual on the Channel Islands"; Ray Corbett, "Chumash Bone Whistles: The Development of Ceremonial Integration in Chumash Society," in *Foundations of Chumash Complexity*, ed. J. E. Arnold (Los Angeles: Cotsen Institute of Archaeology, 2004), 53–62; Sandra E. Hollimon, "The Role of Ritual Specialization in the Evolution of Prehistoric Chumash Complexity," in *Foundations of Chumash Complexity*, ed. J. E. Arnold (Los Angeles: Cotsen Institute of Archaeology, 2004), 113–32.

34. René L. Vellanoweth, Barney G. Bartelle, Amira F. Ainis, Amanda C. Cannon, and Steven J. Schwartz, "A Double Dog Burial from San Nicolas Island, California, USA: Osteology, Context, and Significance," *Journal of Archaeological Science* 35, no. 12 (2008): 3111–23.

35. Perry, "The Archaeology of Ritual on the Channel Islands."

36. Courtney Hofman and Torben C. Rick, "The Dogs of CA-SRI-2: Zoo-archaeology, Diet, and Context of *Canis familiaris* from Santa Rosa Island, California, USA," *Ethnobiology Letters* 5 (2014): 65–76.

37. Hollimon, "The Role of Ritual Specialization in the Evolution of Prehistoric Chumash Complexity."

38. Sandra Hollimon, "Sex, Gender and Health among the Chumash: An Archaeological Examination of Prehistoric Gender Roles," *Proceedings of the Society for California Archaeology* 9 (1996): 205–8.

39. Lynn H. Gamble, "Feasting, Ritual Practices, Social Memory, and Persistent Places: New Interpretations of Shell Mounds in Southern California," *American Antiquity* 82, no. 3 (2017): 427–51.

CHAPTER 6

1. Dewey S. Livingston, "Ranches in the Sea: A History of the Islands within Channel Islands National Park," manuscript on file (Ventura, CA: National Park Service, Channel Islands National Park, 2006); Henry R. Wagner, *Spanish Voyages to the Northwest Coast in the Sixteenth Century* (San Francisco: California History Society, 1929).

2. Lois J. Roberts, "Revising the History of San Miguel Island, California," in *Third California Islands Symposium: Recent Advances in Research on the California Islands*, ed. F. G. Hochberg (Santa Barbara, CA: Santa Barbara Museum of Natural History, 1993), 607–13.

3. Robert Glass Cleland, *From Wilderness to Empire: A History of California* (New York: Knopf, 1959).

4. Wagner, *Spanish Voyages to the Northwest Coast in the Sixteenth Century*.

5. Wagner, *Spanish Voyages to the Northwest Coast in the Sixteenth Century*.

6. Wagner, *Spanish Voyages to the Northwest Coast in the Sixteenth Century*, 239.

7. Wagner, *Spanish Voyages to the Northwest Coast in the Sixteenth Century*, 352.

8. Harry Kelsey, "European Impact on the California Indians, 1530–1830," *Americas* 41, no. 4 (1985): 502.

9. Jon M. Erlandson, Torben C. Rick, Douglas J. Kennett, and Phillip L. Walker, "Dates, Demography, and Disease: Cultural Contacts and Possible Evidence for Old World Epidemics among the Protohistoric Island Chumash," *Pacific Coast Archaeological Society Quarterly* 37, no. 3 (2001): 11–26.

10. Erlandson et al., "Dates, Demography, and Disease."

11. Deana Dartt-Newton and Jon M. Erlandson, "Little Choice for the Chumash: Colonialism, Cattle, and Coercion in Mission Period California," *American Indian Quarterly* 30, no. 3/4 (2006): 416–30.

12. Daniel O. Larson, John R. Johnson, and Joel C. Michaelson, "Missionization among the Coastal Chumash of Central California: A Study of Risk Minimization Strategies," *American Anthropologist* 96, no. 2 (1994): 263–99.

13. Phillip L. Walker and Travis Hudson, *Chumash Healing: Changing Health and Medical Practices in an American Indian Society* (Banning, CA: Malki Museum Press, 1993).

14. John R. Johnson and Sally McLendon, "The Social History of Native Islanders Following Missionization," in *Proceedings of the Fifth California Islands Symposium*, ed. D. Browne, K. Mitchell, and H. Chaney (Santa Barbara, CA: Santa Barbara Museum of Natural History, 2000), 646–53.

15. Johnson and McLendon, "The Social History of Native Islanders Following Missionization."

16. Richard Ellis, *The Empty Ocean* (Washington, DC: Island Press / Shearwater Books, 2003).

17. Ellis, *The Empty Ocean*.

18. Adele Ogden, *The California Sea Otter Trade, 1784–1884* (Los Angeles: University of California Press, 1941).

19. Ellis, *The Empty Ocean*.

20. Ogden, *The California Sea Otter Trade, 1784–1884*.

21. Ogden, *The California Sea Otter Trade, 1784–1884*.

22. Ellis, *The Empty Ocean*.

23. James Bodkin, "Sea Otters," *Alaska Geographic* 27, no. 2 (2000): 74–92.

24. Torben C. Rick, Todd J. Braje, and Robert L. DeLong, "People, Pinnipeds, and Sea Otters of the Northeast Pacific," in *Human Impacts on Seals, Sea Lions, and Sea Otters*, ed. T. J. Braje and T. C. Rick (Berkeley: University of California Press, 2011), 1–17.

25. Todd J. Braje, *Shellfish for the Celestial Empire: The Rise and Fall of Commercial Abalone Fishing in California* (Salt Lake City: University of Utah Press, 2016).

26. Kerry Blankenship Allen, *Island of Cowboys: Santa Rosa Island* (Santa Barbara, CA: Santa Cruz Island Foundation, 1996).

27. Livingston, "Ranches in the Sea."

28. Livingston, "Ranches in the Sea."

29. Don L. Johnson, "Landscape Evolution on San Miguel Island, California" (PhD diss., University of Kansas, 1972).

30. Proclamation of Franklin D. Roosevelt, April 26, 1938, 981.

CHAPTER 7

1. Eric R. Wolf, *Europe and the People without History* (Berkeley: University of California Press, 2010).

2. Ben Goldfarb, *Eager: The Surprising, Secret Life of Beavers and Why They Matter* (White River Junction, VT: Chelsea Green, 2018).

3. Patrick V. Kirch, "Microcosmic Histories: Island Perspectives on 'Global' Change," *American Anthropologist* 99, no. 1 (1997): 30–42.

4. Jon M. Erlandson and Scott M. Fitzpatrick, "Oceans, Islands, and Coasts: Current Perspectives on the Roles of the Sea in Human Prehistory," *Journal of Island and Coastal Archaeology* 1, no. 1 (2006): 5–32; Torben C. Rick, Patrick V. Kirch, Jon M. Erlandson, and Scott M. Fitzpatrick, "Archaeology, Deep History, and the Human Transformation of Island Ecosystems," *Anthropocene* 4 (2013): 33–45.

5. David W. Steadman and Paul S. Martin, "The Late Quaternary Extinction and Future Resurrection of Birds on Pacific Islands," *Earth-Science Reviews* 61, no. 1–2 (2003): 133–47; Stephen Wroe, Judith Field, and Donald K. Grayson, "Megafaunal Extinctions: Climate, Humans, and Assumption," *Trends in Ecology and Evolution* 21, no. 2 (2006): 61–62.

6. Maurice G. Holmes, *From New Spain by Sea to the Californias, 1519–1668* (Glendale, CA: Clark, 1963), 76.

7. Todd J. Braje, Jon M. Erlandson, Kristina Gill, Torben C. Rick, Linda Bentz, and Paul Collins, "Historical Degradation and Ecological Recovery: Evaluating the Marginality of California Island Ecosystems," in *An Archaeology of Abundance: Reevaluating the Marginality of California's Islands*, ed. Kristina Gill, Mikael Fauvelle, and Jon M. Erlandson (Gainesville: University Press of Florida, 2019), 31–58.

8. Don L. Johnson, "Episodic Vegetation Stripping, Soil Erosion, and Landscape Modification in Prehistoric and Recent Historic Time, San Miguel Island, California," in *The California Channel Islands: Proceedings of a Multidisciplinary Symposium*, ed. Dennis M. Power (Santa Barbara, CA: Santa Barbara Museum of Natural History, 1980), 103–21.

9. R. Scott Anderson, Scott Starratt, Benata M. Brunner Jass, and Nicholas Pinter, "Fire and Vegetation History on Santa Rosa Island, Channel Islands, and Long-Term Environmental Change in Southern California," *Journal of Quaternary Science* 25, no. 5 (2010): 782–97.

10. Kristina Gill, "10,000 Years of Geophyte Use among the Island Chumash of the Northern Channel Islands," *Fremontia* 44, no. 3 (2016): 34–38; Kristina M. Gill and Kristin M. Hoppa, "Evidence for an Island Chumash Geophyte-

Based Subsistence Economy on the Northern Channel Islands," *Journal of California and Great Basin Anthropology* 36, no. 1 (2016): 51–71.

11. Patricia M. Corry and Kathryn McEachern, "Patterns in Post-Grazing Vegetation Changes among Species and Environments, San Miguel and Santa Barbara Islands," in *Proceedings of the Seventh California Islands Symposium*, ed. Christine C. Damiani and David K. Garcelon (Arcata, CA: Institute for Wildlife Studies, 2009), 201–14; Steve Junak, Tina Ayers, Randy Scott, Dieter Wilken, and David Young, *A Flora of Santa Cruz Island* (Santa Barbara, CA: Santa Barbara Botanic Garden, California Native Plant Society, 1995).

12. Mariah S. Carbone, A. Park Williams, Anthony R. Ambrose, Claudia M. Boot, Eliza S. Bradley, Todd E. Dawson, Sean M. Schaeffer, Joshua P. Schimel, and Christopher J. Still, "Cloud Shading and Fog Drip Influence the Metabolism of a Coastal Pine Ecosystem," *Global Change Biology* 19, no. 2 (2013): 484–97.

13. Todd J. Braje, Torben C. Rick, Jon M. Erlandson, Laura Rogers-Bennett, and Cynthia A. Catton, "Historical Ecology Can Inform Restoration Site Selection: The Case of Black Abalone (*Haliotis cracherodii*) along California's Channel Islands," *Aquatic Conservation: Marine and Freshwater Ecosystems* 26, no. 3 (2016): 470–81.

14. Torben C. Rick, Robert L. DeLong, Jon M. Erlandson, Todd J. Braje, Terry L. Jones, Douglas J. Kennett, Thomas A. Wake, and Phillip L. Walker, "A Trans-Holocene Archaeological Record of Guadalupe Fur Seals (*Arctocephalus townsendi*) on the California Coast," *Marine Mammal Science* 25, no. 2 (2009): 487–502.

15. Courtney A. Hofman, Torben C. Rick, Jon M. Erlandson, Leslie Reeder-Myers, Andreanna J. Welch, and Michael Buckley, "Collagen Fingerprinting and the Earliest Marine Mammal Hunting in North America," *Scientific Reports* 8, no. 1 (2018): 1–6.

16. Torben C. Rick, "Hunter-Gatherers, Endemic Island Mammals, and the Historical Ecology of California's Channel Islands," in *The Archaeology and Historical Ecology of Small Scale Economies*, ed. Victor D. Thompson and Jamie C. Waggoner Jr. (Gainesville: University Press of Florida, 2013), 41–64.

17. Courtney A. Hofman, Torben C. Rick, Jesús E. Maldonado, Paul W. Collins, Jon M. Erlandson, Robert C. Fleischer, Chelsea Smith, T. Scott Sillet, Katherine Ralls, Wendy Teeter, René L. Vellanoweth, and Seth D. Newsome, "Tracking the Origins and Diet of an Endemic Island Canid (*Urocyon littoralis*) across 7300 Years of Human Cultural and Environmental Change," *Quaternary Science Reviews* 8, no. 15 (2016): 147–60.

18. Paul W. Collins, "Interaction between Island Foxes (*Urocyon littoralis*) and Indians on Islands off the Coast of Southern California: I. Morphologic and

Archaeological Evidence of Human Assisted Dispersal," *Journal of Ethnobiology* 11, no. 1 (1991): 51–81.

19. Timothy J. Coonan, Catherin A. Schwemm, and David K. Garcelon, *Decline and Recovery of the Island Fox: A Case Study for Population Recovery* (Cambridge: Cambridge University Press, 2010).

20. Paul W. Collins, Daniel A. Guthrie, Torben C. Rick, and Jon M. Erlandson, "Analysis of Prey Remains Excavated from an Historic Bald Eagle Nest Site on San Miguel Island, California," in *Proceedings of the Sixth California Islands Symposium*, ed. D. K. Garcelon and C. A. Schwemm (Arcata, CA: Institute for Wildlife Studies & National Park Service, 2005), 103–20.

21. Seth D. Newsome, Paul W. Collins, Torben C. Rick, Daniel A. Guthrie, Jon M. Erlandson, and Marilyn L. Fogel, "Pleistocene to Historic Shifts in Bald Eagle Diets on the Channel Islands, California," *Proceedings of the National Academy of Sciences USA* 107 (2010): 9246–51; Seth D. Newsome, Paul W. Collins, and Peter Sharpe, "Foraging Ecology of a Reintroduced Population of Bald Eagles on the Channel Islands, California, USA, Inferred from Prey Remains and Stable Isotope Analysis," *Condor* 117, no. 3 (2015): 396–413.

22. Rick, "Hunter-Gatherers, Endemic Island Mammals, and the Historical Ecology of California's Channel Islands."

23. Sabrina Shirazi, Torben C. Rick, Jon M. Erlandson, and Courtney A. Hofman, "A Tale of Two Mice: A Trans-Holocene Record of *Peromyscus nesodytes* and *Peromyscus maniculatus* at Daisy Cave, San Miguel Island, California," *Holocene* 28, no. 5 (2018): 827–33.

24. Janet Rizner Backs and Mary V. Ashley, "Evolutionary History and Gene Flow of an Endemic Island Oak: *Quercus pacifica*," *American Journal of Botany* 103, no. 12 (2016): 2115–25.

25. Harold Mooney and Erika Zavaleta, eds., *Ecosystems of California* (Berkeley: University of California Press, 2016).

26. Richard J. Hobbs, Eric Higgs, and James A. Harris, "Novel Ecosystems: Implications for Conservation and Restoration," *Trends in Ecology and Evolution* 24, no. 11 (2009): 599–605.

27. Daniel R. Cayan, Edwin P. Mauer, Michael D. Dettinger, Mary Tyree, and Katharine Hayhoe, "Climate Change Scenarios for the California Region," *Climate Change* 87 (2008): 21–42.

28. Douglas T. Fischer, Christopher J. Still, and A. Park Williams, "Significance of Summer Fog and Overcast for Drought Stress and Ecological Functioning of Coastal California Endemic Plant Species," *Journal of Biogeography* 36, no. 4 (2009): 783–99; A. Kathryn McEachern, Diane M. Thomson, and Katherine A. Chess, "Climate Alters Response of an Endemic Island Plant

to Removal of Invasive Herbivores," *Ecological Applications* 19, no. 6 (2009): 1574–84.

29. Jonathan M. Levine, A. Kathryn McEachern, and Clark Cowan, "Rainfall Effects on Rare Annual Plants," *Journal of Ecology* 96, no. 4 (2008): 795–806.

GLOSSARY

aDNA: Ancient DNA studies are rapidly expanding in archaeology and helping to answer a variety of questions about the evolutionary and genetic histories of plants, animals, and humans. Such research involves recovering genetic material from paleontological, archaeological, and historical materials such as mummified tissues, bone collagen, preserved plant remains, ice cores, marine and lake sediments, and soils.

Anthropocene: A proposed geologic epoch, colloquially called the Age of Humans, recognizing the global impacts of human activities on planet Earth. Proposals for the beginning of the Anthropocene range from roughly 50 years ago (i.e., when radionucleotides entered the atmosphere from atomic detonations), the start of the Industrial Revolution, or as a replacement for the Holocene designation beginning 11,700 years ago.

'Anyapax: The Chumash name for Anacapa Island, which translates to "illusion" or "mirage."

archaeology: The study of the human past from our earliest premodern human ancestors to modern times using material remains. Archaeology has long been an interdisciplinary and collaborative science, which relies on two primary field approaches: (1) *survey*: the systematic investigation of the landscape in search of archaeological sites and (2) *excavation*: the systematic and controlled digging of sub-surface archaeological sites.

Chumash: A Native American cultural group with traditional territories in central and southern California from modern-day Morro Bay in the north to Malibu in the south, along with the Northern Channel Islands. Chumash peoples continue to live in southern California today, with the Santa Ynez Band of Chumash Mission Islands as the only federally recognized of more than a dozen bands of Chumash Indians. Chumash peoples spoke a wide variety of dialects, with the Island Chumash language known as Cruzeño (aka Ysleño and Isleño).

complex hunter-gatherers: This was a term first widely used by archaeologists in the 1990s to distinguish hunter-gather societies with social and economic traits that anthropologists long assumed required agriculture to develop. Complex hunter-gatherers do not rely on domesticated plants and animals for their subsistence econo-mies but exhibit traits such as inherited social inequality, large and dense populations, permanent settlements, and intensive economies focused on wild plants and animals.

conservation biology: A discipline focused on protecting and restoring Earth's biodiversity. Conservation biologists study the distribution of life on the planet, the threats facing life on Earth, and ways to miti-gate the risks and restore ecosystem health and diversity.

deep history: A term referencing the distant past of the human species that extends well beyond the advent of writing systems, integrating perspectives from a variety of disciplines including geology, archaeol-ogy, history, and traditional knowledge.

Early Holocene: A subdivision of the Holocene Epoch typically defined as the time period that began about 11,700 years ago and lasted until 8,000 years ago.

equifinality: The principle that in open, complex systems (such as human cultural systems) a given outcome can be reached by many potential means. In archaeology, this refers to how different historical processes may result in a similar outcome or social formation.

ethnography: The study and description of a particular human society. Contemporary ethnography is almost entirely based on fieldwork and is usually accomplished by a cultural anthropologist immersing himself or herself in the culture and the everyday life of the people who are the subject of inquiry.

ethnohistory: The study of Indigenous peoples using a wide range of historical records and sources, including notebooks and journals, paintings and photographs, sound and video recordings, and much more. There is a rich ethnohistoric record of Chumash peoples including interviews with Chumash descendants and accounts of European explorers, missionaries, and others. These data help us understand a wide variety of Chumash cultural practices, social organization, and ecology.

Gabrieleño-Tongva: A Native American cultural group who historically occupied the Los Angeles Basin and the Southern Channel Islands. While no group has yet gained federal recognition, thousands of Gabrieleño-Tongva people still live in southern California among numerous groups.

geophyte: In botany, a perennial plant such as a potato or blue dick, which propagates in spring from an underground organ such as a bulb, tuber, corm, or rhizome.

Historic Period: For the Northern Channel Islands, the time period from about 1769 CE until the early 1820s, when the Island Chumash were removed or abandoned their island homes and relocated to mainland missions and pueblos. *See also* Mission Period.

historical ecology: An interdisciplinary research program that focuses on the long-term interactions between humans and their environments. Often, historical ecologists apply these century- to millennia-long perspectives of environmental change to modern resource management.

Holocene: The current geological epoch typically defined as beginning at 11,700 years ago, often subdivided into Early, Middle, and Late Holocene divisions based on climatic shifts.

human behavioral ecology: In archaeology, the application of evolutionary theory to the study of past human behavior and cultural diversity. Among other pursuits, human behavioral ecology attempts to explain human behavior as adaptive solutions to meeting the biological needs of humans, such as growth and development, reproduction, and mate acquisition.

isotopes: The variants of chemical elements that possess the same number of protons and electrons but a different number of neutrons. Archaeologists, for example, have used radioactive isotopes to help date past events and stable isotope analyses to document marine climate and reconstruct the diets of ancient humans and other animals.

land bridge: A connection between two landmasses, especially an ancient one that allowed humans and other animals to colonize new territories before being submerged by rising sea levels or other geological processes.

Last Glacial Maximum: A term referencing the most recent time when ice sheets and glaciers throughout the world were at their greatest extent, dated to roughly 20,000 years ago. This was a time when massive ice sheets covered much of North America, Northern Europe, and Asia, profoundly influencing Earth's climate by causing drought, desertification, and a considerable drop in global sea levels.

Late Holocene: A subdivision of the Holocene Epoch typically defined as the time period that began about 4,000 years ago. This period is characterized by the rise of sociopolitical complexity on California's Northern Channel Islands and the adoption of new technologies such as the bow and arrow and the circular shell fishhook.

Late Period: In southern California archaeology, the time period that began about 650 years ago until the first documented contact between the Chumash and Europeans in 1542 CE. During this period, all the hallmarks of Chumash culture (such as plank canoes, intensive nearshore fishing, standardized shell bead currency, ranked societies, and pronounced sociopolitical complexity), recorded by European explorers, were in place.

Limuw: The Chumash word for Santa Cruz Island, which translates to "Place of the Sea."

marine abrasion platform: In geology, a sloping or nearly flat bedrock surface extending out from the foot of a marine cliff, created by wave action and marine abrasion.

marine terrace: In geology, any relatively flat, horizontal, or gently inclined surface of marine origin, bounded by a steeper ascending slope on one side and by a steeper descending slope on the opposite side. Marine terraces are formed by coastal erosion and reflect the history of the rise and fall of sea levels over time.

Middle-to-Late Transition: In California archaeology, the time period that began about 800 years ago and lasted until 650 years ago (1150–1300 CE). This was a time of environmental change in southern California, with fluctuating and unstable ocean temperatures and drier than normal terrestrial conditions and rapid social evolution for the Chumash.

Middle Holocene: A subdivision of the Holocene Epoch typically defined as the time period that began about 8,000 years ago and lasted until 4,000 years ago.

Mission Period: In California, the time period that began in 1769 CE and lasted until about 1833 CE when Spanish colonizers founded 21 missions from San Diego to San Francisco Bay. The missions were established to convert Native Americans to Catholicism and to expand Spanish territory in the New World. *See also* Historic Period.

NAGPRA: The Native American Graves Protection and Repatriation Act is a 1990 federal law that provides for the repatriation and disposition of Native American human remains, funerary objects, sacred objects, and objects of cultural patrimony. NAGPRA requires that tribes be consulted when archaeological investigations encounter or expect to encounter Native American cultural items or when such items are unexpectedly discovered on federal (such as within Channel Islands National Park) or tribal lands.

Paleocoastal: A term used to refer to the earliest coastal occupants of the Americas. The Paleocoastal complex corresponds with Paleoindian, Clovis, Folsom, and other peoples in the interior of the North American continent. On the Channel Islands, the Paleocoastal period occurs from more than 13,000 years ago to 8,000 years ago and includes chipped stone crescents, Channel Island Barbed points, and other tools.

Pleistocene: A geological epoch typically defined as the time period that began about 2.6 million years ago and lasted until about 11,700 years ago. The Pleistocene was the most recent of the Ice Age climatic events, when glaciers covered large parts of Earth and large mammals (megafauna) such as mammoths and mastodons roamed North America.

Protohistoric Period: A division of time often used by archaeologists to refer to the period between first contact of European colonial powers with Indigenous cultures and the establishment of permanent colonial settlements. For Northern Channel Islands archaeology, the Protohistoric Period refers to the time interval between the arrival of Cabrillo in 1542 CE and the establishment of the first California mission in 1769 CE.

Quaternary: The most recent period of the Cenozoic Era. The Quaternary includes the Pleistocene and Holocene epochs from roughly 2.6 million years ago to the present day.

radiocarbon dating: A method for determining the age of carbon-based materials, such as organic material or animal remains, by measuring the amount of carbon-14 present in a sample compared against a reference standard. Radiocarbon dating is the most common chronometric dating technique used by North American archaeologists to build local cultural histories.

restoration: In ecology, restoration is the process of assisting in the recovery of an ecosystem that has been degraded, damaged, or destroyed by natural or anthropogenic events.

Santarosae: The super-island of Anacapa, Santa Cruz, Santa Rosa, and San Miguel islands coalesced into a single landmass during cold Ice Age intervals, when sea levels were considerably lower than they are today.

shell midden: More generally referred to as "middens," this is a common archaeological site type consisting of shells, animal bones, botanical remains, and artifacts that are the refuse of past human activities.

shifting baselines: In biology and ecology, this term refers to the situation where over time knowledge is incrementally lost about the state of the natural world because people do not recognize or perceive the changes taking place.

stable isotopes: The analysis of stable isotopes (nonradioactive forms of atoms), especially carbon, nitrogen, oxygen, and strontium, is a crucial part of archaeology and historical ecology. The analysis of stable isotopes from these and other elements found in archaeological, historical, and modern bones, shells, teeth, and other tissues can help reconstruct ancient diet, food webs, ecosystems, climate, migration patterns, and more.

tomol: The Chumash term for sewn redwood plank canoes used to travel from island to island and from the mainland to the islands both historically and today.

Tuqan: The Chumash name for San Miguel Island and a primary Chumash village on San Miguel Island.

Wima: The Chumash name for Santa Rosa Island that translates to "driftwood."

RECOMMENDED FURTHER READING

THE CHUMASH OF SOUTHERN CALIFORNIA

Blackburn, Thomas C., ed. 1975. *December's Child: A Book of Chumash Oral Narratives*. Berkeley: University of California Press.

Gamble, Lynn H. 2008. *The Chumash World at European Contact: Power, Trade, and Feasting among Complex Hunter-Gatherers*. Berkeley: University of California Press.

Hudson, Travis J., and Thomas C. Blackburn. 1982–1986. *The Material Culture of the Chumash Interaction Sphere*. Vols. 1–5. Menlo Park, CA: Ballena Press.

GENERAL INTEREST CALIFORNIA ARCHAEOLOGY

Arnold, Jeanne E., and Michael R. Walsh. 2010. *California's Ancient Past: From the Pacific to the Range of Light*. Washington, DC: Society for American Archaeology.

Fagan, Brian. 2004. *Before California: An Archaeologist Looks at Our Earliest Inhabitants*. Walnut Creek, CA: AltaMira Press.

Gamble, Lynn H., ed. 2015. *First Coastal Californians*. Santa Fe, NM: School for Advanced Research Press.

CHANNEL ISLANDS ARCHAEOLOGY

Arnold, Jeanne E., ed. 2001. *The Origins of a Pacific Coast Chiefdom: The Chumash of the Channel Islands*. Salt Lake City: University of Utah Press.

———, ed. 2004. *Foundations of Chumash Complexity*. Los Angeles: Cotsen Institute of Archaeology, University of California.

Braje, Todd J. 2009. *Modern Oceans, Ancient Sites: Archaeology and Conservation of San Miguel Island, California*. Salt Lake City: University of Utah Press.

———. 2016. *Shellfish for the Celestial Empire: The Rise and Fall of Commercial Abalone Fishing in California*. Salt Lake City: University of Utah Press.

Gill, Kristina M., Mikael Fauvelle, and Jon M. Erlandson, eds. 2019. *An Archaeology of Abundance: Reevaluating the Marginality of California's Islands*. Gainesville: University Press of Florida.

Glassow, Michael A., ed. 1993. *Archaeology of the Northern Channel Islands of California: Studies of Subsistence, Economics, and Social Organization*. Salinas, CA: Coyote Press.

Glassow, Michael A., Jennifer E. Perry, and Peter Paige. 2008. *The Punta Arena Site: Early and Middle Holocene Cultural Development on Santa Cruz Island*. Santa Barbara, CA: Santa Barbara Museum of Natural History.

Grenda, Donn R., and Jeffrey Altschul, eds. 2002. *Islanders and Mainlanders: Prehistoric Context for the Southern California Coast and Channel Islands*. Redlands, CA: Statistical Research.

Jazwa, Christopher S., and Jennifer E. Perry, eds. *California's Channel Islands: The Archaeology of Human-Environment Interactions*. Salt Lake City: University of Utah Press.

Jones, Terry L., and Kathryn Klar, eds. 2010. *California Prehistory: Colonization, Culture, and Complexity*. Walnut Creek, CA: AltaMira Press.

Kennett, Douglas J. 2005. *The Island Chumash: Behavioral Ecology of a Maritime Society*. Berkeley: University of California Press.

Laverty, Corinne H. 2019. *North America's Galapagos: The Historic Channel Islands Biological Survey*. Salt Lake City: University of Utah Press.

Raab, L. Mark, Jim Cassidy, Andrew Yatsko, and William J. Howard. 2009. *California Maritime Archaeology: A San Clemente Island Perspective*. Walnut Creek, CA: AltaMira Press.

Rick, Torben C. 2007. *The Archaeology and Historical Ecology of Late Holocene San Miguel Island*. Los Angeles: Cotsen Institute of Archaeology, University of California.

Rick, Torben C., and Leslie A. Reeder-Myers. 2018. *Deception Island: Archaeology of 'Anyapax, Anacapa Island, California*. Washington, DC: Smithsonian Scholarly Press.

HISTORICAL ECOLOGY

Crumley, Carole L., ed. 1994. *Historical Ecology: Cultural Knowledge and Changing Landscapes*. Santa Fe, NM: School of American Research Press.

Crumley, Carole L., Tommy Lennartsson, and Anna Westin, eds. 2017. *Issues and Concepts in Historical Ecology: The Past and Future of Landscapes and Regions*. Cambridge: Cambridge University Press.

Isendahl, Christian, and Daryl Stump, eds. 2019. *The Oxford Handbook of Historical Ecology and Applied Archaeology*. Oxford: Oxford University Press.

Jackson, Jeremy B. C., Karen Alexander, and Enric Sala, eds. 2012. *Shifting Baselines: The Past and the Future of Ocean Fisheries*. Washington, DC: Island Press.

Kittinger, John N., Loren McClenachan, Keryn B. Gedan, and Louis K. Blight, eds. 2014. *Marine Historical Ecology in Conservation: Applying the Past to Manage for the Future*. Berkeley: University of California Press.

Pauly, Daniel. 2019. *Vanishing Fish: Shifting Baselines and the Future of Global Fisheries*. Vancouver, BC: Greystone Books.

Siegel, Peter E., ed. 2018. *Island Historical Ecology: Socionatural Landscapes of the Eastern and Southern Caribbean*. New York: Berghahn Books.

HISTORICAL RANCHING ON THE NORTHERN CHANNEL ISLANDS

Chiles, Frederic Caire. 2015. *California's Channel Islands: A History*. Norman: University of Oklahoma Press.

———. 2017. *Justinian Caire and Santa Cruz Island: The Rise and Fall of a California Dynasty*. Norman: University of Oklahoma Press.

Eaton, Margaret Holden. 1980. *Diary of a Sea Captain's Wife: Tales of Santa Cruz Island*. Edited by Janice Timbrook. Charlotte, NC: Mcnally & Loftin.

Ehrlich, Gretel. 2000. *Cowboy Island: Farewell to a Ranching Legacy*. Aptos, CA: Santa Cruz Foundation.

Gherini, John. 2015. *Santa Cruz Island: A History of Conflict and Diversity*. Norman: University of Oklahoma Press.

Healey, Pete. 2017. *The Island: Reminiscences of Twentieth-Century Ranching on Santa Rosa Island*. Los Olivos, CA: Healey Enterprises.

Lester, Elizabeth Sherman. 1974. *The Legendary King of San Miguel: Island Life in the Santa Barbara Channel*. Charlotte, NC: Mcnally & Loftin.

Roberti, Betsy Lester. 2008. *San Miguel Island: My Childhood Memoir, 1930–1942*. Aptos, CA: Santa Cruz Foundation.

INDIGENOUS CULTURES OF CALIFORNIA

Akins, Damon B., and William J. Bauer Jr. 2021. *We Are the Land: A History of Native California*. Berkeley: University of California Press.

Anderson, M. Kat. 2013. *Tending the Wild: Native American Knowledge and Management of California Natural Resources*. Berkeley: University of California Press.

Heizer, Robert F., ed. 1978. *Handbook of North American Indians*. Vol. 8, *California*. Washington, DC: Smithsonian Institution Press.

Lightfoot, Kent G., and Otis Parrish. 2009. *California Indians and Their Environment: An Introduction*. Berkeley: University of California Press.

Margolin, Malcolm. 2017. *The Way We Lived: California Indian Stories, Songs, and Reminiscences*. 2nd ed. Berkeley, CA: Heyday Books.

Panich, Lee M. 2020. *Narratives of Persistence: Indigenous Negotiation of Colonialism in Alta and Baja California*. Tucson: University of Arizona Press.

INDEX

Abalone Rocks estuary, 54, 68

Age of Humans. *See* Anthropocene period

Alta California, 79, 112, 114–15, 118

American Galápagos, 2, 20

American oystercatcher, 7

Americans, 119

Anacapa Island (*'Anyapax*), 1, 2, 3; as Channel Islands National Park, 135; Late Holocene settlements on, 80–81, 83; lighthouse on, 133; marine terrace on, 25; as National Monument, 7, 134–35; in public domain, 133; ranching on, 134; structures on, 133–34; volcanic rock in, 23

Anderson, Scott, 71

animals. *See* fauna

'antap, 102–3, 106

Anthropocene period, 32–33, 156–58, 160

anthropogenic climate change, 156–58, 160

'Anyapax. See Anacapa Island

'aqi, 107

archaeology, 8, 13; Abalone Rocks estuary, 54, 68; animal remains in, 49, *49*; anthropogenic climate change and, 160; bald eagle nest sites in, 153; CA-SMI-87 site, 80–81; CA-SMI-163 site, 99, *100*; CA-SRI-666 site, *56*, 56–60; Chinese abalone fisheries in, 124; conservation and, 7–8, 144–45, 147, 150, 153; human diet in, 93–94, *94*; Middle Holocene, 56, *56*, 58, 59–60; Native Americans, federal law and, 84; NPS and, 144–45; Paleocoastal, 41–45, *43*, *44*, 51; ranching in, 128–30, *129*; sea level rise in, 157, 160. *See also* historical ecology; human remains; shell midden

"The Archaeology of Channel Islands Ranching" (Perry & Buchanan), 128–30

Civil War, 126

clams, 68

climatic events, 85–86. *See also* anthropogenic climate change

Clovis, 27, 37, 38–40, 45, 52

Coastal Migration Theory, 39–40

colonialism, 6, 11, 17, 108; Native Americans and, 138; by Spaniards, 114–15

conservation: agency efforts in, 7–8, 141, 158; anthropogenic climate change and, 156–58, 160; archaeology and, 7–8, 144–45, 147, 150, 153; bald eagles in, 153–54; black abalone in, 149–50; Chumash in, 144–45, 158–59; CINMS in, 7, 135, 141, 144, 147, 159; of endemic animals and plants, 151–56, *155*; fox in, 152–54; goals, ecological changes and, 141–42, *143*, 145; historical amnesia in, 11–12; historical ecology and, 15–17, 139, 141–43, *143*, 153–54; historical perspectives in, 7–8, 13; hope, change and, 158–60, *159*; marine ecosystems in, 147–48; MPAs in, 135; NPS in, 128, 135–36, 141, 142, 144–45, 147, 150, 153; red abalone in, 147–49; Roosevelt on, 134–35; seals and sea lions in, 150; shifting baselines syndrome in, 11–13; terrestrial and marine ecosystem goals in, 145–50; TNC in, 7, 136, 141, 142, 144, 153, 158, 159

Cook, James, 8, 11, 118

Cordero, Alicia, 5–6

crescents, *43*, 52; artistry of, 50; at Daisy Cave, 42; disappearance of, 55, 57; on San Nicolas Island, 3; on

Santa Catalina Island, *3*; on Santa Rosa Island, 46

Daisy Cave, 30, 38, 41, 59–60; crescents at, 42; Paleocoastal technologies in, *47*, 47–48

Darwin, Charles, 8–9, 140

deer mouse, 31, 154

DeLong, Robert, 150

Diaz, Sue, 5–6

diving, 64

DNA research, 72–74, *73*, 93–94

dogs, domesticated: burial of, 106–7; introduction of, 54, 74–75

dolphin, 67, 69–70, *70*, 99

dunes, 53, 131, 157; in Early Holocene period, *34*, 34–35; in Pleistocene period, 29–30

Eaton, Ira K., 134

ecosystem: beavers in, 138–39; modern impact on, 139; Native American management in, 137–39; shifting baselines syndrome in, 11–13; terrestrial and marine, 145–50. *See also* historical ecology; island ecology

endemism: deer mouse in, 31, 154; foxes in, 151–53; plants in, 154–56, *155*; subspecies in, 152

English, 119

Erlandson, Jon M., 41, *49*, 57–58; "Island Chumash Rock Art" by, 103–5, *104*; "People and Plants on California's Channel Islands" by, 100–101; "Stone, Asphaltum, and Freshwater Resources of the Northern Channel Islands" by, 22–23

erosion. *See* sea level

Californians by, 115; Ferrer with, 111–12; livestock grazing, ecology and, 116; Manila Galleon trade by, 112, 113; Mission period of, 114–18; missions, Mexican government and, 117; missions, slavery and, 116; Old World diseases, Chumash and, 114, 115; Portolá with, 115; Serra with, 115, 116; Vizcaíno with, 112–13

"Stone, Asphaltum, and Freshwater Resources of the Northern Channel Islands" (Erlandson), 22–23

stone shrines, 105–6, *106*

subsistence: ecology, human health, Chumash and, 93–102, *94, 100*; for Paleocoastal period, 48–50, *49*

survey, 42

Sutton, Elizabeth, 81

tar seeps, 22, 23

Tchunashngna. See Santa Barbara Island

technology: exchange, Late Holocene period and, 87, *87*–93, *90*; first Islanders changing of, 55–57, *56, 62*; of fishing, 90–91, 95; of Paleocoastal period, 42, 45–48, *47*; sedentism, mobility, Middle Holocene period and, 55–62, *56, 61. See also* tools

Tecolote Point, 58–59

TNC. *See* The Nature Conservancy

tomols, 87, *87, 90*, 93; annual crossing by, *159*, 159–60; Brotherhood of the Tomol, 88–89, 102; description of, 78, 88; harpoons and, 90–91

tools, 41, *43*; birds in, 99; bone in, 46–47, *47*, 55, 60; bow and arrow,

87, 91–92; chert in, 22–23; donut stones, 60, *61*; fishhooks, 47, *47*, 87, 91; harpoon, 87, 90–91; from Late Holocene, 80–81; lithic scatters of, 42–43; from Middle Holocene, 56–57, 60, *61*; mortar and pestle, 60; red abalone in, 63. *See also* artifacts; beads; boats; Channel Island Amol points; Channel Island Barbed points; crescents

Torrey pine, 33, 155, *155*

trade, 112–13; bead currency in, 22, 23, 87, *87*, 92–93; by Chumash, 22–23, 50, 93; fur, 75

Transverse Ranges, 20–21

Tuqan. See San Miguel Island

United States Navy. *See* military, US

Vail and Vickers Company, 127–28, 129, 136

Valenzuela, Diane, 5–6

Vasquez, Veronica, 5–6

Vellanoweth, René L., 89–90, 106–7

Ventura Basin, 24

Vizcaíno, Sebastian, 112–13

volcano, 10, 21, 23

Waiya, Luhui Isha, 5–6

Walker, Phillip, 85, 96

Wallace, Alfred Russel, 9, 140

Waters, William G., 131–32

Webster, H. Bay, 133–34

"Were Humans and Mammoths on the Channel Islands at the Same Time?" (Muhs), 27

wetlands, 30

Wima. See Santa Rosa Island

ABOUT THE AUTHORS

Todd J. Braje is professor of anthropology at San Diego State University with specialties in long-term human-environmental interactions, the archaeology of maritime societies, historical ecological approaches to understanding coastal hunter-gatherer-fishers, and the peopling of the New World. Braje has conducted archaeological and historical ecological research on the Northern Channel Islands for nearly 15 years and worked at sites ranging from 12,000-year-old lithic workshops to 19th-century Chinese abalone fishing camps. Braje has published two other books on Channel Islands archaeology and history, most recently *Shellfish for the Celestial Empire: The Rise and Fall of Commercial Abalone Fishing in California* (2016).

Jon M. Erlandson is the executive director of University of Oregon's Museum of Natural and Cultural History. He has worked on the Channel Islands for nearly 40 years and studies the origins and development of maritime societies, human dispersals, the peopling of the Americas, historical ecology, and the history of human impacts on marine fisheries and ecosystems. His field research focuses on California's Channel Islands, but he has also worked extensively along California's mainland coast, the Oregon coast, in Alaska, and in Iceland. Erlandson has published 20 books and more than 300 scholarly articles. In 2013, Erlandson was elected a fellow of the American Academy of Arts and Sciences.

Torben C. Rick is curator of Human Environmental Interactions and North American Archaeology in the Department of Anthropology at the Smithsonian's National Museum of Natural History. Rick's research focuses on the archaeology and historical ecology of coastal and island peoples, especially on the North American Pacific and Atlantic coasts. He has active field projects on California's Channel Islands, Santa Barbara County mainland, and the Chesapeake Bay that investigate ancient and modern human environmental interactions. Rick (along with Leslie A. Reeder-Myers) recently published *Deception Island: Archaeology of 'Anyapax, Anacapa Island, California* (2018).